# Amish Miller Twins Amos & Andy

## Childhood and Young Adult Years

**Amos J. Miller**



Twin Rose Publishing
22128 County Road 28
Goshen, IN 46526

***Amish Miller Twins Amos & Andy: Childhood and Young Adult Years***



**ISBN 0-9721583-9-1**

Front Cover Art: Betty Jean Miller
Back Cover Art: Angel Schultz
Page Design & Layout: GET Printing

Printed by GET Printing, 432 Blackport Drive, Goshen, IN 46528
Printed in the United States of America

*Amish Miller Twins Amos & Andy* by Amos J. Miller and *Memories of Faith* by Alma Bontrager may be ordered from Twin Rose Publishing. To order or request information, please call or write:

**Twin Rose Publishing** **574-875-3911**
**22128 County Road 28**
**Goshen, IN 46526**

# *Dedication*

To the memory of my ancestors and grandparents, Urias E. and Rebecca (Yoder) Miller and Emanuel E. and Elizabeth (Miller) Bontrager and my parents, John U. and Susan E. (Bontrager) Miller. It is through their zeal for that which is right, and because of the upbringing I experienced, that I am now enjoying many blessings.

To the present generation. I hope to leave an influence in such a way that it may tend to further their eternal welfare.

To generations yet unborn, I also dedicate this first book about Amos and Andy. May they also have the privilege of looking back to an ancestry which has been true to man and to God. Trusting that although not perfect, this book may be useful and interesting and will instill within us a proper regard for our ancestry. May it cause us to aim to do our part in giving our own posterity a worthy ancestry to look back to.

I dedicate this book to all those who may read it. May it be a blessing in their lives.

*"May the Lord add His blessing to this book; may it strengthen an inner conviction in the hearts of many. May they be called to a bold yet humble life in the Lord Jesus to demonstrate the seemingly lost vision of the Prince of Peace to a dying world. Amen."*

—Amos J. Miller

# Contents

## Part II – Young Adult Years

# *Preface*

Our father and mother are John U. and Susan E. (Bontrager) Miller. John U. Miller was born on January 12, 1910 in Shipshewana, Indiana. Susan E. Bontrager was born on November 1, 1909 in Thomas, Oklahoma. John and Susan (Sue) were married in Indiana on November 26, 1931 by Mose H. Lehman. Their first home was in the Shipshewana area.

Our family moved onto the Floyd Haller farm on March 30, 1939. The farm is located four miles east of Topeka, Indiana, then one-quarter mile north, the first farm on the right. Our two older brothers were born before the move. Emanuel was born on October 28, 1932, followed by Ezra on May 28, 1935.

My twin Andy and I were born on Tuesday, June 13, 1939. soon after the move to the Haller farm.

On March 8, 1945, another son, John Jr. was born. Two brothers were born before us twins and died as infants. A sister was stillborn after us.

After the family moved to Iowa, another brother, Johnathon, was born on September 5, 1946. My parents have six of us boys living.

The first four years covered in this book are based on information obtained from my parents and from their journals. The balance is written from memories and from old letters which were used to date actual happenings.

*Amish Miller Twins Amos & Andy: Childhood and Young Adult Years* shares the life journey of the "Amish Miller Twins" and our family from 1939 to 1962. A second Amos & Andy book will cover the next 40 years of our lives.

I want my twin brother, Andy, to know that I love him very much. It is my hope that we can be drawn closer together through the sharing of these experiences. After all the hurts we have gone through, I hope that our love for each other will grow stronger.

If anyone's life is changed by reading this book, it would be a blessing to hear from you.

–AJM

## *Special Thanks*

First of all, I want to thank Alma Bontrager for the long hours she spent on this book, editing and putting it into story form. Alma's first published book is *Memories of Faith*. From her experience, Alma has been able to share with me, also the author of my first book. Alma's second book is at its beginning stage, as is the second Amos and Andy book. (Alma's books are available through Twin Rose Publishing.)

Many thanks to Angel Schultz for sharing her God-given art talent. She drew the portrait for the back cover from an old photo taken by a distant relative. She also is the artist of the illustration of the farm where we were born.

Thanks to my wife, Betty Jean, for the special art on the front cover. As I directed her, she drew things important in our life. The little wagon, a favorite in my childhood. Two roses to represent twins. The small stream, a near drowning. The windmill on Grandpa's farm, cold water. The heart-shaped flower bed, our love for each other.

I also want to thank all those who helped in many ways to make this first Amos & Andy book possible.

With sincere thanks,
Amos

## Our Grandpa — Urias E. Miller
***Excerpts from His Journal***

**Feb. 1, 1939** – Levi took a load of wood to Ligonier.
**Feb. 6, 1939** – The boys cut some more logs. Poplar wood $30 per thousand - Red oak $35 per thousand.
**Feb. 11, 1939** – Buzzed wood for other people in their woods.
**Feb. 24, 1939** – Grandpa took hogs to town sold four at the yards got $7.60 each.
**March 2, 1939** – The boys tapped some maple trees.
**March 9, 1939** – They gathered maple water and boiled it. The following days we sold 20 gal syrup for $1.50 gal.
**March 23, 1939** – They gathered the maple pails and the balance of the maple water and finished boiling it.
**April 4, 1939** – Urias took two cords wood to Ropp duck farm. Urias and Lizzie planted potatoes. We got 60¢ per cord.
**April 8, 1939** – John bought a team of horses west of Topeka for $70 each. *[This is the twins' father.]*
**June 13, 1939** – Johns had twins this eve Johns had twins. *(Written twice and underlined—guess Grandpa was kind of proud of the twins Amos & Andy.*
**June 14, 1939** – We went to John's this Wed. evening to see the twins.
**June 18, 1939** – Grandma stayed at John's over Sunday and also stayed Monday and Tuesday to help with the twins.
**Aug. 28, 1939** – Sold twelve bushel peaches at 95¢ per bushel.
**Aug. 31, 1939** – Andy started school in AM – in PM he dragged the fields. We all went to John's in the evening.
**Sept. 8, 1939** – We made 11 gal apple butter today.
**Nov. 9, 1939** – Grandpa and Grandma went to John's for dinner. In PM Grandpa went to Ralph Weber's sale eight miles east of Topeka.
**Dec. 19, 1939** – Grandpa & Grandma went to John's, Grandpa went to Topeka sale to buy sows, got two red ones for $16 each, one darkest one for $14.75 and black Jim for $13.

**Dec. 23, 1939** – Took eight hogs to town, got 5¢ lb. for them.
**Dec. 29, 1939** – Grandma & Lizzie were up to Topeka and to John's. Grandpa went to Shipshewana, the boys worked in the woods.

It appears our Grandpa cut logs and firewood for income and sold maple syrup, peaches and hogs.

# Our Father — John U. Miller
## *Excerpts from Ledgers and Journals*
## *1932 – 1945*

### Dad's Ledgers

***Income***
Eggs 8¢ - Cream 18¢ lb. - Potatoes 43¢ per bushel - Chickens 5¢ per lb. - Calves 55¢ per lb. - work for other farmers 10¢ per hour - Sheared Sheep 17¢ per head

***Expenses***
Workshirts 58¢ - Work Shoes $1.85 - Size 7 Shoe for Emanuel 78¢ - New Oilstove $14.50 - Maytag Washer $79.50 - Quarter Beef $6.08 - qt. milk 5¢ - 10 lb. sugar 45¢ - Bed Springs $6.50 - thread 10¢

### Dad's Journals

**June 13, 1939** – Cultivated all day, it was nice all day. In the evening twin boys arrived in our home named Amos & Andy.
**July 30, 1939** –Today we were in church at Noah J Miller's. This is the first Sunday we took the twins to church.
**Nov. 23, 1940** – Mom took Andy to Doctor, he got sick with pneumonia.
**Dec. 15, 1940** – Today we were at home all day, Amos and Andy were sick.
**Feb. 6, 1941** – Mom and the twins went to Iowa with Joe Hostetler.
**Feb. 20, 1941** – Mom and twins came home from Iowa trip OK.
**July 13, 1941** – Dad - Emanuel & Ezra went to church, Mom stayed home with the twins as they were exposed to the measles.
**Aug. 5, 1943** – Mom took Amos & Andy to dentist in Topeka.
**March 9, 1944** – Amos started with scarlet fever.
**Dec. 25, 1944** – Amos got sick today.
**Dec. 30, 1944** – Andy is a lot better - he had rheumatic fever.

**March 8, 1945** – Today a baby boy arrived here to stay with us. I helped take care of him. It was 2/0 and everything was frosty, the baby's name is John Jr.
**March 31, 1945** – Today Dad took Amos & Andy to Topeka and got them each a pair of shoes.
**July 24, 1945** – Mom took Andy to doctor in Topeka.
**Oct. 12, 1945** – Today Sue - Jr and I left for Iowa to look for a place. My folks stayed with the rest of the children.
**Oct. 24, 1945** – We returned from our trip to Iowa.

These excerpts tell some of the things our parents went through with their twin sons.

## *About the Author*

Amos J. Miller was known as the writer in the family, along with his mother. Susan wrote many letters to *The Budget* until her death in 1981.

When Amos attended Triumph School, the teacher had given his class an assignment: "Write a story." It didn't have to be a true story, but one could be made up. Amos ended up with the "number one story" in his class. The teacher and the class thought Amos's story was true, but he told them that it was "only a made up story." The teacher told Amos that he should think about being a writer.

Amos Miller is an individual who has compassion for others. He says, " I am so thankful for the Biblical convictions and principles that my parents instilled in us while we were growing up. As the author, my desire is that those who read the story of the Amish Miller twins, may be moved to allow God to enter into their lives and receive a blessing."

# Amish Miller Twins
# Amos & Andy

## Part I — Childhood

Chapter 1

# Big News

The sun was shining brightly on this particular June morning as John and Susan Miller got out of bed. John quickly dressed and headed out the door toward the barn. There were chores to be done.

As Susan was dressing, she thought to herself, "I think this will be a special day." She slipped her dark-colored dress over her bulging tummy. She had been extra big during this pregnancy, and the due date was drawing near. Before starting breakfast, she woke up seven-year-old Emanuel and four-year-old Ezra.

When John came in an hour later after chores, Sue had fried mush and tomato gravy waiting to be served. After breakfast the boys went outside, and Sue whispered to her husband. "John, the baby has been moving around a lot this morning. I think, maybe, this is that special day! Maybe you'd better go over to Dan Yoder's to see if the boys could stay there if need be."

"Sure, I'll do that," came John's reply. "And maybe you should call Dr. Hilderbrand to check on me." "Sure, I'll do that too," John answered. He got up, hugged his wife, and walked out the door. He hitched up a horse and made his way over to Dan's. Then he stopped at a neighbor's to call the doctor. Coming back into the house, he found Susan in pain.

Dr. Hilderbrand arrived that afternoon, but soon left. He had informed Susan, "Call me if things get worse."

The pains kept Susan from doing any household chores. Around nine o'clock that evening, Susan decided it was time to call the doctor back. John took the boys to Dan's and then called the doctor.

"But why are we spending the night at Dan's?" little Emanuel asked his dad. "We'll have a big surprise for you when you get home in the morning," John answered.

The doctor arrived shortly, and Susan's water broke. Checking things out, the doctor encouraged the couple, "It shouldn't be long now!" A few minutes later he announced, "Well, look at this, a nice baby boy!" Some time had gone by and the doctor was taking care of the baby when Susan said, "Doctor, I'm having pains again."

The doctor looked over at Susan and said, "Yes, Mrs. Miller, that's natural. You'll have some afterbirth pains."

"No. This is something different, Doctor."

Dr. Hilderbrand wrinkled his brow into a frown. He went on cleaning up the baby until he heard a gasp coming from Susan.

"Are you okay, Mrs. Miller?" he asked in concern.

"I don't know, something just doesn't feel right," Susan answered as she wiped the perspiration from her brow.

"Just a minute, I'll check things out," the doctor said while handing the baby to John.

As he turned to check on his patient again, Susan had another pain—and another baby entered the world!

The doctor gasped in astonishment, "Well, I'll be! We've got us another boy!" Now all three were amazed at the "surprise baby."

"Never has this happened to me before in my years of practice!" Dr. Hilderbrand exclaimed. He was almost as excited as John and Susan.

"I've always known beforehand when twins were to be born, but this was a surprise!"

"No wonder I gained so much weight this time!"

John's voice came next, "Dear, what will we name these twins?"

"Oh, yeah, they need names!" laughed Susan. "Well, we had picked out Amos for a boy." After some thought, they decided the names should be Amos and Andy.

"Could I take pictures of the twins?" asked the doctor. Shaking his head, John cleared his throat and answered, "We would rather you didn't, as it's against our belief."

Dr. Hilderbrand showed disappointment, but he tried to understand and respect their religion.

"Who did you name the twins after—the comedy show's Amos and Andy?" the doctor asked.

"No, we've named them after relatives, Uncle Amos and Uncle Andy." They also explained to the doctor that both were biblical names from the Bible.

Dr. W.O. Hilderbrand had been delivering babies in Amish homes for years. He just didn't think when he asked them about the popular radio show. The doctor knew there were no radios in Amish homes.

Now came a problem, the babies looked identical.

"How are we going to tell them apart?" asked John, concerned.

"Maybe Dr. Hilderbrand could put bands on their arms," said Susan.

"Sure, I can do that."

The next morning, John hitched up the horse real early and drove to the Yoder residence. They all were at the kitchen table enjoying their breakfast.

"Good morning, John!" called Dan as John entered the kitchen.

"Good morning, everybody!" he said, looking at his sons. "Well, we have that big surprise now."

"What's the surprise, Dad?" asked Emanuel.

"We have twin boys!"

"Mama has a baby?" asked Ezra.

"She has two babies," answered John.

"Mama has a . . . a . . . TWO babies?" asked Ezra again. He could hardly believe his ears. Usually mothers had only one baby! Wow! Two babies to love. Scooting his chair back, he asked, "Can we go home now?" He was anxious to see those babies.

"Well, eat your breakfast first, then we'll go."

It didn't take the boys long to finish, and they thanked the Yoders for letting them stay.

John and Susan had a hired maid to help them out, but even then they had their hands full. They still enjoyed the twins and said, "We wouldn't want it any other way."

The arrival of the twins had made news in the local paper. The Millers received lots of gifts from relatives and the local stores for which they were thankful.

When the twins were about a year old, Emanuel and Ezra would babysit while John and Susan did the chores.

On one particular evening, Susan came in from milking finding Amos by himself on the floor. He had reached in behind to his filled diaper, helping himself! Picking up Amos, she called to the boys, "Emanuel, Ezra!"

"Yes, Mom," they answered from the other room. They came running after hearing their mother's voice!

"Didn't I tell you to watch the babies?" Looking at each other, then back to their mother, they nodded their heads in shame. They got carried away with a game and forgot to watch the babies.

"Look at what a mess Amos has gotten into! When your dad gets in here, you'll need a little discipline!"

As Susan was changing Amos's diaper, he wet on Andy's head. Now Mother had to clean up Andy too.

Emanuel and Ezra were sorry now for not doing their job. But it was too late. That night John made two trips to the woodshed.

John and Sue were proud parents. Already, Amos seemed to always be the "leader." Yes, John and Susan had their hands full but wouldn't have traded the twins for anything in the world.

**Floyd Haller Farm – twins born here**

Chapter 2

# Accidents and Sickness

It was a nice summer day with temperatures in the upper 80's. Before supper John took Emanuel, Ezra, and the twins back to the river to swim and bathe.

While John was bathing Andy, he called to his eldest son, "You boys watch out for Amos while I bathe Andy."

After finishing with Andy, he called out, "Okay, Amos, your turn! Emanuel, where is Amos? I'm ready for him."

Emanuel and Ezra had been so busy swimming and playing. they had forgotten about Amos. Looking around, they spotted Amos floating down the river.

John gasped at the sight of his son—and then Amos was gone again. Taking off on the run, he called to the boys, "Watch Andy while I go find Amos!"

Coming to the spot where he had last seen Amos, John called out, "Oh, Amos, where are you?" Then he saw Amos again up ahead. The water got deeper, making wading more difficult for John—desperately trying to get to his son. Tears streamed down John's face as he prayed, "Oh, Lord, please let me get to Amos before it's too late." Now Amos had gone down for the fourth time, "Lord, am I too late?" John asked in a sob. Finally, after what seemed like an hour, he reached his son. He carried the limp form to the riverbank. "Emanuel, run for help!" John called back to his eldest son.

Holding Amos upside down, he patted his back. Water poured from the lad's mouth, nose, and ears. Just as John was ready to give up, Amos let out a cry!

"It's okay, Amos," he reassured his five-year-old son. Relief swept over John as he heard his son's whimpers.

"Thank you, Lord," John prayed now as he heard the ambulance arrive. The ambulance crew checked Amos out. They assured everyone Amos would be fine.

"You did the right thing, Mr. Miller," they had said.

This experience stayed with Amos for the rest of his life. His fear of water stayed with him forever.

That night Susan remarked, "You know, I think the Lord spared Amos's life for a special reason. I think he must have something special for his future." They were all grateful that Amos was alive.

One morning, as Susan started out to the chicken house to butcher chickens, she called out to Ezra, "You watch the twins while I'm butchering."

"Okay, Mom," he called back. The twins had been playing out behind the corn crib, so Ezra went to find them.

After some time Susan called to Ezra again, "Can you take these chicken wastes out and dump them?"

"Sure, Mom," came the reply. He obeyed his mother's orders and returned the bucket to her in the chicken house.

Back outside again, he heard a question. "What happens to the chicken wastes?" asked the twins.

"You don't know what happens to that stuff?" Ezra asked mischievously.

"No," came the double reply.

"Well. . .er. . .you see," Ezra stuttered, "if you go over to the far corner you can watch the Indians come up from the woods and take it. They eat stuff like that."

"No they don't," said Amos.

"You just go and see if they don't!"

Amos and Andy obeyed their brother but didn't expect anything to happen.

As they hunched back in the corner, Ezra let out a big Indian war cry. Both boys froze as they looked at each other in shock. The Indians were here already! They both took off running for the house as fast as they could go so the Indians couldn't get them.

As they came barreling into the kitchen, white as a sheet, Mother asked, "What on earth has happened?" Trying to catch their breath, Amos finally answered, "Mom . . . there's an Indian . . . out by the corn crib . . . taking the chicken scraps!"

"Now, boys, boys, there are no Indians out there."

"Yes, Mom, we heard them holler," came Andy's shaky voice. "Come and we'll show you."

Taking the lead, Susan took the frightened boys to the corn crib. Just then Ezra came out of the crib.

"Ezra," came Susan's voice, "did you tell the twins there are Indians out here?"

"Er-r-r, em-m-m. . . ," Ezra cleared his throat. "Yes, Mom, I did. I was only having fun." He knew the fun was over now.

"Ezra, now that wasn't nice. You know better than that. I guess when Dad comes home, I'll let him deal with you."

Ezra did not look forward to seeing his pa come home that night, but that ended the Indian attacks from then on.

The day was Sunday, and as the twins tired of playing in the sandbox, Amos said," Andy, come here with me, let's play on the cultivator."

"Dad said we're not supposed to go on there," came Andy's reply.

"We won't break anything. You be my horse, and I'll act like I'm cultivating." Binder twine served as lines for Amos's horse.

After a while Amos grew tired of his pretend cultivating. Stepping down from the seat, he slipped and rammed his side into a sharp blade. Hanging there, Amos let out a loud scream. Andy ran for help.

"Mom, Dad, come quick! Amos is hurt on the cultivator!" screamed Andy.

"The cultivator?" asked John, heading for the door in big strides.

"We were playing on the cultivator, and Amos got hurt."

Reaching the cultivator, John lifted Amos up and out. Blood was oozing from the large wound. Carrying his son to the house, he was met by Susan on the porch.

"How bad . . . uh . . . is . . . he?" Susan turned pale and felt faint.

John put Amos down and caught his wife just as she fell. Now he had two people to take care of. What next?

"Emanuel, hold this handkerchief on Amos's cut while I tend to your mother."

John ran inside. Grabbing a cold washcloth, he ran back outside and held it to Sue's forehead. She stirred and opened her eyes. "What happened?" she asked. "Oh, yeah . . . Amos . . . is he all right?"

"Now don't you worry none about Amos," John said, trying to comfort his wife. "Can you get me some clean, white cloth? Now don't look at Amos, or you might faint again."

"Emanuel, run to the neighbor's to see if they can take us to the hospital with Amos."

Amos was in great pain. He was sorry he had disobeyed his father's orders for not playing on the cultivator.

At the hospital, when the doctor applied the needle to numb the wound, Amos let out a big scream. The doctor needed to put eight stitches on the inside and fourteen on the outside.

For punishment, John took away Amos's favorite toy for a week. Amos was very sorry he had not listened. He thought the wound was punishment enough.

The summer went fast, and soon fall was upon the Millers.

One day Andy grew ill and lay around in bed. Each day he grew worse. John and Sue couldn't understand what ailed their son. They kept hoping he would soon get better. This was also hard on Amos because he didn't have Andy to play with. Several times when Amos went up to his bed, Andy let out a cry. "Don't touch my bed," he would cry out. Amos couldn't figure out why Andy would scream in pain like that. After all, he wasn't cut.

Andy was taken to the doctor and diagnosed with rheumatic fever. It took several months for Andy to get back on his feet again. After that Andy's health was never the same. Amos tried to look out for his twin brother and protect him.

For Christmas that year, John and Susan bought the boys a new Radio Flyer sled. John had made a wooden sled for hauling wood for the stoves in the house. One Sunday afternoon, the boys, Emanuel, Ezra and the twins, took the sleds out for some fun. Emanuel and Ezra took the new sled, and the twins settled for the homemade sled.

"Emanuel, can you push me?" begged Amos.

"Just a minute," came the reply.

Awhile later, Amos was on his way down the hill on the homemade wooden sled.

"Wow, this is fun!" Amos hollered back to his brothers. But the next thing he knew, he was headed for some trees at the bottom of the hill.

CRASH! Amos's nose came down hard on the sled. "WHA-a-a-a-a-a-a—" Amos let out a long, loud scream.

Scrambling down the hill, the other boys went to Amos's rescue. "Are you okay?" asked Andy.

Amos just kept on screaming and ran for the house! Blood was oozing from his nose.

Running ahead, Ezra called, "Mom, Dad, come here! Amos is hurt."

Opening the door, Susan took one look and backed away. She would let John take care of this. Feeling faint, she went to sit on a chair while John appeared on the scene.

"Why does that boy always get hurt?" Susan wondered.

Taking a look at his son, John administered a cold rag until the bleeding stopped. Taking a good look, he said, "Well, Amos, I think we have a broken nose here!"

"What?" came the frightened lad's voice.

"Yes, sir, Amos, I think so."

"Well, it sure feels like it," Amos answered.

"Now you boys tell me what happened," said John looking at his two older sons.

After they told their father how they were sledding, they knew they were in trouble.

"Now Emanuel and Ezra, you knew better than to let the twins ride the homemade sled."

Both boys dropped their heads in shame. Yes, they should have known better.

"I guess maybe sledding is over for the rest of the day," John's voice echoed in the stillness of the room.

"Yes, Dad," came Emanuel's voice.

Amos had learned another lesson the hard way!

Chapter 3

# Memories of Indiana Years

Susan's brother, Ezra Bontrager, entered the Army in November 1942 at the desert training center in California. While there, he had a young girlfriend from Texas. He spent a total of nine years in the Army. Much of his time was spent as a chief cook.

One day, Susan walked to the mailbox thinking, "I hope I have some letters today."

Opening the lid, she let out an excited squeal. "Hurrah! A letter from brother Ezra," she said out loud. She didn't even wait until she got to the house to open it. Carefully unfolding the letter, she read . . .

May 23, 1943

Dear Sis,

Thought I would drop you a few lines to let you know I'm fine and hope you are the same. We just got back from the mountains last night, was there a week. Received your package and that maple syrup was very good.

We had command raids the other night and we won. The hand grenades were made out of flour and sand. Our commanding officer thought we did a fine job. My buddy and I were at Los Angeles a week ago and three black guys jumped us, took our money and watches. So I guess we will have to stay in camp until next payday.

Don't know much to write, so will close.

As ever,
Bro Ezra

Tears flowed down Susan's cheeks as she went into the house. Reaching into the pocket of her faded, well-worn dress, she withdrew a tattered hanky. How she wished Ezra had never joined the Army. The house was quiet, so she found her way through the kitchen, living room, and on to their bedroom through blinding tears. Sobbing, she knelt at the side of her bed and silently prayed, "Oh, Lord, please be with brother Ezra as he lives in danger. Please protect him as he goes on through this life."

Susan let out a deep sigh and dabbed at the last, flowing tears. She felt better now. Getting to her feet, she made her way to her desk to find some paper. She needed to write to him again.

When John and the boys came in for dinner, Susan shared the letter from her brother.

"Sounds like he's living in danger," commented John. Susan only nodded her head in agreement.

A few weeks later another letter arrived.

June 11, 1943

Dear Sis,

Received your much welcome letter. I am still kicking as usual and hope you are the same. I got a letter from sister Mattie yesterday. I average one letter a day, but wouldn't care if I got 3 or 4 a day. I always like to hear from home.

About a furlough, they offered me ten days. That wouldn't hardly be long enough and then there is the matter of money.

I am sending one of my Army pictures to sister Mattie, maybe if you ask her, she will send it to you so you can see what a real soldier looks like, ha.

With love and best wishes,
Bro Ezra

More letters followed in the weeks to come.

February 9, 1944

Dear Sis and Family,

Received your letter you wrote in January and was glad to hear from you again, also got a letter from bro Noah today. I'm glad you are better again. I'm all right.

Thanks very much for sending those books. I am still in the kitchen. I have a chance of taking a correspondence course in German. It is a college course, so I might be able to make something out of it.

Will close for this time

Love and Best Wishes

Bro Ezra

Another letter found its way to the Miller mailbox from Germany.

March 8, 1944

Dear Sis and Family,

I received your letter you wrote on February 23 a few days ago and was glad to hear from you again.

My mail has been awful slow lately, airmail letters is all I have been getting. I will probably get a dozen letters all at once one of these days, that's the way it usually goes.

Say Sis, I didn't think about it at the time, if it takes some of your points to get handkerchiefs, please don't get them. I can get along without them. Hope everybody is well, I am Okay. Weather has been nice lately. Well I must close for now.

With Love,

Ezra bye

Susan wrote this for *The Budget* years later . . .

On March 2nd 1951, we received the sad news that my brother Ezra Bontrager was killed on February 28 in a car and train wreck in Heddesheim, Germany. It took patience in waiting for his body to arrive at Kalona, Iowa. From the time of his death until the day of the funeral was 29 days. We had not expected that the coffin would be opened for us to view him, but to our surprise they opened the coffin and he was in perfect condition. He looked like a person that had died only a day or two before, so we cannot be thankful enough to the authorities that they fixed him in such a way that he stayed in such good condition so long.

We found out since that they fix the dead bodies over there so they will keep well for 90 days. There was a glass cover on the coffin under the lid. There was only one little scar on his face that we think was caused in the wreck. An Army escort accompanied Ezra's body to the Kalona funeral home, but did not stay for the funeral.

I have now written this much, hoping it might be of some benefit to some people sometimes who have relatives in foreign countries, as life is so uncertain that nobody knows which one in the family is next, one across the sea or one from this side of the sea.

Mrs. John U. Miller

In the newspapers, Ezra's obituary read . . .

SFC Ezra Bontrager, son of Emanuel E. and Elizabeth (Miller) Bontrager was born January 22, 1920 near Centreville, Michigan. Died February 28, 1951 in Heddesheim, Germany at the age of 31 years, 1 month and 6 days.

Ezra died of cerebral edema incurred when a privately owned car he was driving collided with a train at a railroad crossing. Funeral services were held March 29, 1951 at 10:00 AM at the Fairview Conservative Church near Kalona, Iowa. Conducted by Elmer G. Swartzentruber and Albert Miller.

Surviving are his deeply bereaved fiancee Elizabeth Czemals of Burlafinger, Germany, his Father and Stepmother of Middlebury, Indiana and the following brothers and sisters. Joni, Lovina, Susan Fairbank, Iowa, Fannie Miller Middlebury, Indiana, Menno Bontrager Sturgis, Michigan, Mattie Miller Kalona, Iowa, Noah New Castle, Indiana, half sister, Alma, and half brother, Amzie of Middlebury, Indiana.

Before entering the service, he had been employed in the Smith Cafe in Iowa City, Iowa.

He entered the Army in November 1942, spending the last six years of his life in and around Heidelberg, Germany. To our knowledge, he never was in action. Much of his time was spent as a chief cook.

As we loved him, so we miss him
In our memory he is dear
Loved, remembered, though as always
Brings many a silent tear.
We do not know what pain he bore
We did not see him die
We only know he passed away
And we could not say good-bye
-by two Sisters

Times were hard during the years of World War II. The men had to go away for years to serve in hospitals and in other non-military jobs far away from their homes and communities. Some young Amish men also went into the military as noncombatants. The families greatly missed their sons and grandsons.

Everywhere at that time, there were shortages of material things. Some things you couldn't buy at all. Some food was rationed. Books of ration stamps were issued for set quantities of food to be used for a set time for each person in the family. Stores gave little tokens as "change" to customers when a purchase didn't use up an entire ration stamp.

Sugar could be bought only with the ration stamps. To substitute for hard-to-get sugar, homemade maple syrup was used. Susan would remind her sons, "That's enough syrup, boys!" Amos thought he needed enough syrup to hold his cereal together!

The twins enjoyed going to Grandpa Miller's. Their lane seemed a mile long to the twins. Grandma Miller made taffy from maple syrup. The taffy would melt in your mouth. The syrup was cooked in a large tank inside a log cabin. The twins also enjoyed helping themselves to the rows of grapes and to fresh fruit from their grandparent's orchard!

Grandpa had a large cow barn so the boys enjoyed watching Grandpa with the cows. Susan would remind the boys to help clean the barn out. The twins would rather play so they hid so Mother wouldn't see them. They would gather the eggs though, because that was something they loved to do.

What looked like an airplane propeller going around could be seen at the top of the hog house. That windmill furnished lots of cold water.

Grandpa also had a furniture shop. Amos found it fascinating to watch his Grandpa shape the wood into different pieces of furniture.

In the winter months, the twins would carry wood for the wood boxes. There were two to keep supplied.

One day at home, Amos and Andy were playing in the horse barn when Amos came upon some dried-up horse droppings. The horses had been out to pasture for quite some time, so these dropping had hardened. Picking up a hard-ball dropping, Amos said, "Here Andy, taste this, they're good!"

"No, they're not!" came the quick reply.

Pretending to munch on the ball, Amos said, "Sure they are."

Taking the ball, Andy looked at it several times, and then looked back to his brother.

"Go ahead, they're good," Amos pretended to still be chewing on one.

Taking a bite, Andy choked, "Ugh!" He gagged at the awful taste. "Amos, I'm telling Mom!"

Amos knew he was in trouble as he saw Andy turn and run for the house.

Andy was back soon and said, "Amos, Mom wants to talk to you!" Slowly, Amos made his way to the house.

"Amos Miller, you know better than that!" came his mother's stern voice. She spanked Amos soundly. Amos was sorry for playing the trick on Andy, but it was too late. He would need to be more careful after this.

One summer evening, the boys had been playing tag by the bank barn when Ezra jumped down and landed on a 2x4 with spikes sticking up out of it. The spikes were embedded in Ezra's heel. Ezra screamed until his dad had the board removed. Ezra limped around for a few days.

This was to be the last summer spent in Indiana.

On Monday, January 28, 1946, the Millers had an auction. And on Monday, February 4, 1946, the trucks were loaded to move to Buchanan County in Iowa. The next morning, the family traveled by Greyhound bus to their new location.

What would the future hold for the Millers?

Chapter 4

# New Beginnings

The morning of February 6, 1946 brought the Millers to Independence, Iowa. The weather was snowy. Word was received of one truck's breakdown which meant it wouldn't arrive until the next day.

Lots of people came to help unload when the truck arrived. The day was cold with lots of snow. The Millers would be renting the farm from Susan's sister, Lovina, and her husband, George. This was the Duffy Farm.

George's lent the Millers some cows, and they purchased more to make a herd of ten. That would help to keep the boys busy.

Time went fast and soon it was time to sow oats. This was done by using a spreader. The spreader was attached to the back of the grain wagon with a chain going into the sprocket in the wagon wheel. In Indiana, oats would be drilled into the ground instead of spread. John had part of the oats spread when he discovered he had the mumps. The neighbors then came in and finished sowing the oats for him.

George's daughter, Fannie, came over to help Susan for a while.

One morning, Amos woke up with a swollen throat. "Mom, I think Fannie gave me the mumps!"

"Now Amos, I want you to know Fannie didn't have anything to do with you getting the mumps," Susan assured her son.

Fannie stayed on for two weeks helping out at the Miller's. The twins helped to wash dishes and do other household chores.

By spring, Emanuel and Ezra started going to Fairbank School. The roads got so muddy that the bus got stuck. John helped it out several times with his team of horses. For a few weeks, John would drive the boys two miles to meet the bus until the roads got better.

Andy had been stirring the milk on the stove to pasteurize it for one-year-old baby Johnny. He stood on a wooden block in order to reach the kettle better. Andy happened to get too close to the edge of the block and it tipped over—bringing down the kettle of hot milk over his arm and body! Andy let out screams and wailed in pain.

Susan quickly took Andy out in the cold air and called for her husband. They used scissors to cut away the sleeve, and when they laid it open, the skin on his arm came off too. The doctor was called right away and arrived as soon as possible.

Taking a quick look at his patient, the doctor said, "Mr. Miller, I'm afraid your son needs to be hospitalized."

Susan pleaded with him, "Please, just tell me how to care for him here, and I can do it myself."

The doctor looked up in surprise. "The courage of this woman," he thought. "Are you sure you can manage?" he asked.

"Yes, Sir, I'm sure," came the confident reply.

The doctor made a sling, and put Andy's arm and hand into it. He then tied Andy's arm to a chair. A pan was placed under his arm to catch the fluids that drained off. A few days later, the arm got to looking real bad, so the doctor was called again. He made several trips to see Andy, each time bringing something different to try on the arm. Amos felt bad for Andy. He now had a double load of chores to do. He missed having his brother up and around.

The twins' sixth birthday was arriving, bringing more responsibilities such as mowing lawn, watching brother Johnny, garden work, and always canning to help Mom with. Play time was limited down to zero—so it seemed to the twins.

Summer passed into August.

By fall, potatoes were dug by John and the older boys while the twins came along and picked up the harvest. Sweet corn was also on the list. The twins would help their mother bring it in, and then they would husk it. All this hard work helped them to grow up, even if at times they didn't think so.

The twins would go after the milking cows in the evenings. On one particular evening, Amos took Maggie, the farm dog, with him to fetch the cows. The farm bull ran with the cows. The bull had a blinder halter on so the bull had only downward vision. That evening, Amos noticed the blinder was partly off Mr. Bull.

"Oh, no," Amos muttered, to himself and to Maggie, as he saw the bull coming for him. Taking off, he headed for the nearby cornfield. Just as Amos got to the fence, the bull was there too. The bull stepped on Amos's leg.

"Maggie!" Amos yelled. "Sick 'em!"

Maggie came running, barking, and landed on top of the bull! She kept on barking and biting at the bull's head until he moved enough to free Amos. Amos then slid under the fence and ran into the field far enough so he couldn't see the bull.

"Come here, Maggie," he called as his little heart pounded within his chest. Maggie came running.

"Thanks, Maggie. Now you go back and take the cows home to Dad."

Maggie was obedient to her training and took the cows home, barking, and nipping at their heels. The cows seemed to be so stubborn that evening!

John was anxious, waiting for Amos to return with the cows. "He should have been here already. It isn't like Amos to not have the cows here on time."

"Emanuel and Ezra, maybe you should go see what's going on. It's not like Amos to take so long," called John concerned about the matter.

"Okay, we will," said Emanuel taking off for the pasture field. Finding their way to the back pasture, they stopped in their tracks. "Ezra, look at the bull!"

"Oh, no," cried Ezra. "Where is Amos?"

The bull was still pawing the ground where Amos had crawled beneath the fence.

"Amos! Where are you?" Emanuel called after his brother.

Peeking his head out of the corn stalks, Amos answered, "I'm here in the corn! The bull came after me, so I hid in the cornfield."

"Come with us, Amos. We'll take you on up to the house."

As Amos followed his brothers to the barn, he poured out his story of the bull attacking him.

That night, Maggie got lots of attention. She was praised for saving Amos's life. And Mr. Bull got his blind halter fixed and a ring in his nose with a four-foot chain attached! After that ordeal, Susan insisted one of the older boys always go along to fetch the cows.

The twins were supposed to mow lawn one hot summer day, but oh, it was so hot! It felt good to sit under the cottonwood trees to cool off. Sitting there enjoying the shade of the beautiful trees, they heard a buzzing sound. Looking up, they saw bees going in and coming out from a hole in the tree.

"Andy, what would happen if we poked a stick in their hole?" asked Amos, looking up the tree, then back to his brother.

"Hm-m-m . . . I don't know," came the answer. "Maybe they would buzz a little louder."

Amos would poke around in the hole, and then they would both run until the bees settled down again. This was fun until all at once a whole swarm of bees came after the boys! They ran for the house, but Amos didn't make it. The bees buzzed in his face and hair causing him to scream in pain from their awful stings.

Andy entered the house with a few bees after him. He called out, "Mom, Amos has a bunch of bees on him!"

Grabbing a broom, Susan ran outdoors finding Amos rolling around on the grass. Swatting at the bees, they finally killed enough for Amos to get up. What a sight! Taking Amos into the house, she fetched a comb and combed more bees out of his hair. Amos was hurting real bad by now. A short time later, Amos complained, "Mom, my head aches real bad." By that time, he couldn't keep his balance. Then he passed out. He eyes were swollen shut.

Susan was thinking . . . if Amos got stung so many times, the poison could kill him. "Ezra," Susan called after her son. "Would you go call a doctor for Amos? Hurry!"

When the doctor arrived, he gave Amos a shot and removed the stingers.

As soon as John heard about the bees attacking Amos, he went out to investigate them. A large swarm had gathered on a branch about half way up the tree.

"Maybe Dan Mast would want those bees for his hives," he said to his family. "I think I'll go see him tonight yet."

Dan came over right away. Setting up his ladder, dressed in his "bee suit," he climbed up with saw in hand. Just as he was ready to bring the branch with the bees down, the branch he stood on broke. Down came Dan with a crash.

"John," Dan called out. "I've broken my arm and leg, I think!"

"Stay right there, and I'll call an ambulance," came John's sympathetic voice. "What next?"

Dan was taken in the ambulance to the hospital still wearing the bee suit. He needed to stay a few days.

John found a board and nailed it across the bees' hole in the tree. The bees had done enough damage for one day!

A few days later, Amos and Andy were found pounding the board so they could hear the buzzing again. Guess what happened when John found out? The rest is history!

**Duffy Farm**

Chapter 5

# Lost Brother — School Days

"Amos! Andy!" came Susan's voice as she sorted the clothes in preparation for washing.

"We're in the sandbox, Mom," echoed Amos from outside.

"I want you boys to watch Johnny while I do the washing."

"Just bring him out here," answered Andy still busy digging in the sand with a shovel.

All that morning, Johnny and the twins played hard in the sandbox. "I'll show you how I can build a sand castle," said Amos to his brothers.

"Boys, it's dinnertime, come in and wash up," called Susan from her kitchen window.

"Dinnertime? Doesn't seem like we've played very long," said Andy. Amos picked up Johnny and headed for the house. He was hungry.

After dinner, the twins did dishes while Susan put Johnny down for his nap. After that they were free to play again until chore time.

A few hours later, Mother brought Johnny outside again to play. "You watch him real good while I do my ironing," Susan said, bringing Johnny over to the sandbox.

Finishing the ironing, Susan sighed. "How I wish they'd make material that wouldn't need to be ironed," she thought to herself. "But then, I shouldn't complain, because I'm just glad I have all these clothes." Putting the ironing board back in the closet, she decided to get Johnny because it was time for the twins to do chores.

"Amos and Andy," she called as she approached the sandbox, "where is Johnny?"

"What? Oh, er . . . Johnny?" came Amos's worried voice. "I don't know what happened to him."

"We forgot to watch him," Andy replied with sorrow in his voice. They knew they were in trouble now.

"Help me look for him," came Susan's plea.

"Johnny, Johnny," they called as they looked in the barn and all through the other buildings. But there was no answer.

"Where did you boys see him last?"

"I'm not sure, Mom," answered Amos.

"Well, go get your dad and the other boys to help us find him."

Amos didn't think his eighteen-month-old brother could get very far. Surely he was somewhere nearby. By now John had come in to help in the search.

"Emanuel, you and Ezra go to the neighbors and ask them if they could help look for Johnny," John told his two sons. While they were gone, John told his wife, "You know maybe Maggie could help us find Johnny."

"I'll run in and get some of his clothes." Susan was soon back.

With some persuasion, Maggie sniffed the clothes, then the ground. She took off for the road, crossed it and headed for the cornfield.

"Maggie! Come back here!" yelled John. Maggie returned to her master, and they started over again. John let Maggie sniff the clothes again. She headed for the road.

"Do you think he's really in there?" came Susan's worried voice. Only a few hours of daylight remained.

Neighbors were gathering by now. They all agreed to help search the cornfield. The corn being about five feet high made it difficult to see down the rows.

Susan decided to stay at the end of the cornfield in case Johnny would come out on his own. Tears formed in her eyes as the others left in search of her baby. "Lord," she prayed, "please let them find the baby. If not, please protect him from harm." Closing her eyes again for just a minute, she asked the Lord to give her strength in whatever lay ahead. The sun was sinking fast.

"Looks like I'll have to go back and get some lanterns and flashlights," said John in a weary voice. How he hated to turn back.

"We found him," came a neighbor's voice. Little Johnny was fast asleep between the rows of corn.

"Run on up and tell your mother we found him," John said to Emanuel. Emanuel ran as fast as he could.

"Mom, Mom, we found Johnny!"

Relief swept over Susan. John carried his son out of the cornfield to his waiting wife. Handing the lad over to Susan, John saw her tears spill on his little head as she hugged her baby. John and Susan thanked the Lord for his safety.

John and the boys resumed their chores as Susan took Johnny to the house to fix their supper.

After supper was over, John and Susan talked to the twins about the responsibilities of babysitting. What if little Johnny had been hit by a car when he crossed the road? The concerned look on Mother's face was enough punishment for the twins. After that they tried hard to understand the seriousness of responsibilities. Amos was glad for such an understanding, loving mother.

In the fall of 1946, the twins were ready to start school at the age of seven. They were so excited about riding the school bus.

It wasn't long until one evening, Amos remarked to his mother, "The other children in school are so dumb!"

"Why Amos Miller, you shouldn't say such things!" came Susan's voice.

"Well, they are because we can say our ABC's and count up to a hundred, and they can't."

"That doesn't mean they're dumb, Amos. They haven't had anyone to teach them those things yet. And remember, you are seven years old, and they are six."

"Why are we a year older when we start school?" asked Amos.

"Then when you get to the eighth grade, you don't need to go to the high school," Susan answered with concern.

Amos didn't understand all this. Why, school was so much fun why wouldn't a person want to go on to high school? He did understand now that it was wrong to say the other students were dumb. His mother made that quite clear!

The school term ended too soon for the twins. They had enjoyed every minute of kindergarten. At the end of the term, their teacher, Mrs. Mabel Dingsley, made a trip to the Miller home.

Susan invited the teacher in and they chatted about everyday things first. Then came a question, "Mrs. Miller," the teacher cleared her throat, "I came to talk to you about Amos and Andy."

"Now what have they done?" thought Susan.

"I think they should be promoted to the second grade. They are ahead of all the other pupils, and I really don't find it necessary for them to go into the first grade. We could begin the first semester in second grade, and if it doesn't work out we can always put them back in first."

Relief flowed through Susan as the teacher finished her little speech.

"I have no objection to that, but I shall ask my husband and we can let you know what we decide," said Susan, happy that the twins were doing so well.

Mrs. Dingsley got up to leave thanking Susan for her time. "It was a pleasure meeting you, Mrs. Miller," she said, extending her hand.

The second grade went well for the twins. Their teacher was Mrs. Amber Ford.

A girl named JoAnn Bradley was a good friend to Amos. He thought she was a beautiful girl. A "girlfriend" in the eyes of Amos. One day JoAnn didn't come to school and Amos missed her. He asked the teacher, "Where is JoAnn today?"

Mrs. Ford looked up at Amos. She swallowed the lump in her throat. Clearing her throat she said, "Amos, come sit down, I need to talk to you."

Amos could tell something was very wrong. Mrs. Ford seemed so sad as she talked. Obeying, Amos found a seat nearby.

"Amos, I'm sorry to have to tell you this," tears formed in her eyes now, "JoAnn and her sister were killed in an automobile accident last night."

Amos's heart beat wildly and tears flowed down his cheeks.

"I know, Honey, it's hard isn't it?" the teacher said. As she hugged Amos, she pulled out a handkerchief from her pocket and wiped the tears from the boy's face.

"But think, Amos, JoAnn is in Heaven now."

Amos had a hard time keeping his mind on schoolwork the rest of that day. Tears kept blinding him. Coming home from school that night, he poured his little heart out to his mother.

"Mama . . . ," he started in as soon as he found her alone in the kitchen preparing supper. Looking up Susan was startled to find her son close to tears. "Are you okay, Amos?" she had asked.

Shaking his head yes, he started again, "Mama, JoAnn Bradley, a girl from our class was killed last night." By now the tears were running down his cheeks. Laying aside the potato she was peeling, Susan wiped her hands on her apron and squatted down to her son's level.

"I'm sorry, Amos," she said as she took his shoulders in her hands.

"I liked JoAnn a lot, Mom," cried Amos. Patting the child's back, Susan wondered how she could comfort her son.

"Her sister died too," came the sobbing voice.

"How sad, but Amos you know Jesus took those girls to Heaven. If we love Jesus and receive Him in our hearts, we too can go to Heaven when He calls us home. Then we can be with the Bradley sisters as well as our other loved ones who have gone before us." Susan wiped her son's tears with her apron and then dabbed at her own eyes.

Amos felt better already, now that he had shared this with his mother. He knew Mother would show her love and concern and comfort him.

✧ ✧ ✧

In 1997, I went to Iowa to acquire pictures of all the schools we twins had attended. First, I went to Fairbank School, the school where we started.

As I got out of the van at Fairbank, a man was standing on the sidewalk. He asked if he could help me. I told him I didn't know if the building was still being used or not, and that I started school here fifty years ago. I told him I was from Nappanee, Indiana, and was here to get a picture of the schoolhouse for a book I was writing—a book about the Amish Miller twins, Amos and Andy.

The man introduced himself and said he was from Kokomo, Indiana originally, and he is the music teacher here. He then invited me into the school, and said he would have one of the teachers take me on a tour. I told him I didn't want to bother them, but he insisted that it was no bother.

Once inside the school, he introduced me to some teachers and informed them what I was doing and that I started school here fifty years ago. You talk about getting royal treatment, I sure did and felt quite honored to be there. One of the teachers took me to the classrooms and showed me the library where the stage used to be.

I asked the teacher if she would have known a girl by the name of JoAnn Bradley. She informed me that she had only been with the school system for three years.

She told me there were several rooms with pictures on the walls. I could look at them if I wanted to. After looking to see if I could find JoAnn's picture, with no success, I decided to leave. Before I left, the teachers said they would be honored to have my book in their library. I told them I would see to it that they got one.

When I left the school, I felt uplifted. They were so kind to show me around.

Then I went downtown to a soda fountain. It used to be a drugstore years ago. It was 10:00 a.m., so I thought I would have some coffee. There was only one person there, a gray-haired lady who was the owner. She asked if she could help me, so I told her I just wanted some coffee.

When she brought me the coffee, I told her what I was doing here. I don't know why, but I thought she might know something about JoAnn Bradley. I asked her if she would have known a girl by the name of JoAnn Bradley in 1947? With a surprised look, she said yes, she knew her. I said, you did? I was getting excited that I found someone who knew her. Then she told me that JoAnn was her sister. You talk about an awesome feeling, it was like I had gone back in time.

We sat there and talked for about an hour. She told me that her sister Carolyn was just younger than she was, and Carolyn was driving when she and JoAnn were killed.

As I left, I thanked her for taking time to talk to me. I don't remember the woman's name, guess I was taken too much by her being JoAnn's sister.

**Fairbank School**

Chapter 6

# Another Brother — Log Cabin

The end of summer 1946 brought with it a bountiful crop of potatoes, onions and carrots—all of which needed to be harvested and put up for winter storage. There was little free time for the twins.

Susan had written Grandpa Millers in Indiana that the birth of a grandchild was near. A few weeks later, another son came to join the Millers. They named him Johnathon. The twins were delighted to have another baby around. But it did bring more chores and work along too. They all pitched in and helped each other. The twins would sometimes fuss as to whose turn it was to hold and feed baby brother Joni. Then Susan would step in and let them know whose turn it was.

December was upon them and with it came wood cutting time. Wood was cut a year in advance so it could dry out. It was called curing. John had bought a team of white horses the past summer which they named Fritz and Betz. This was the first winter the twins were allowed to go wood cutting.

Mr. Simmons lived six miles from the Millers. He gave them permission to cut wood on his land. Six to eight foot long logs were cut, hauled with bobsled across the river, and piled.

"Dad, I heard the ice crack," Amos said in alarm.

"Now Amos, there's two feet of ice on there and it won't break," John assured his son. Amos still wasn't so sure about all this.

After about a week of hauling logs, the neighbors came to help "buzz" them into smaller pieces. Then they were thrown on wagons and bobsleds to be hauled to the farm.

Amos enjoyed hearing the echo of his axe chopping away the branches on a clear crisp morning.

"Whose echo do you think that was?" Amos would ask his brothers. This went on as a game until John said, "Okay, boys, time to get moving—no more games!"

The boys also took turns with the crosscut saw. The saw was about five feet long with a handle on each end. One person at each end pulled back and forth until the wood was cut through.

John would say, "Don't push down on the saw, you'll make it catch. Let the weight of the saw do the work." Even on a cold zero morning, it wouldn't take long to get warmed up when you were working the saw. The coats and jackets were soon shed.

The real treat came at noontime. A log cabin was nearby which provided a fireplace. About an hour before time to eat, one of the boys would run up to the cabin and start the fire. When it was time to eat, the cabin was warm, and their lunches were warmed up in the fireplace.

Susan would prepare the lunches in the mornings for them to take along. The lunches contained canned hamburger, bread, milk, and cookies.

The twins were so cold by the time they reached home in the evening, they could hardly walk. They would be excused from chores, but Susan would ask for their help preparing supper which often consisted of soup or cornmeal mush. What was left of the cooked mush would be fried the next morning and served with gravy.

The wood-making days held a lot of good memories for the twins, but they were always glad when it was time to retire for the night. Oh, that lumpy old mattress felt good!

"We're going to Jake Plank's today," John announced to the boys one Sunday morning at the breakfast table.

"Goody!" the twins chorused. They loved to go visit on their in-between Sunday. They took a team hitched to the double buggy.

After having a good time at Jake's, it was time to head back home and get to those chores.

"Amos, you and Andy go get the team out will you?" asked John.

"Sure, Dad," came the answer and their dad headed for the barn. Bringing out the team, Amos led them around the buggy. Other friends were also getting ready to leave and were hitching up their horses to the buggies. All of a sudden, a friend's horse picked up his two hind feet and kicked out back intending to get one of Amos's horses. They missed their aim and caught Amos square in the chest. Amos flew fifty feet back under another buggy. He lay unconscious for a while.

A neighbor was summoned to take Amos to the hospital where X-rays were taken. Internal bleeding was found in the chest area plus two hoof prints that were black and blue already. Amos was kept overnight for observation. He never got over the fear of the "rear location of a horse" after that.

"Why does everything happen to me?" Amos wondered.

One night Emanuel and Ezra were excused from the chores with instructions to keep an eye on the younger boys. Playing different games led Emanuel to deciding to swing Amos around in circles by holding on to his head. After a few circles, Amos went limp. Putting him down and letting go, Emanuel could see Amos had passed out.

"Amos, wake up," he pleaded as he shook Amos. Amos lay limp as a rag. Leaving Amos, Emanuel ran to the barn for help.

"Mom, Dad, come quick, Amos has passed out!"

"What in the world happened now?" asked Susan as she headed for the house. Shamefully, Emanuel explained the situation.

Amos was again taken to the hospital by a good neighbor. Amos finally came around at the hospital. Checking him thoroughly, the doctor told the Millers that Amos had a vertebra out, which pinched a nerve causing him to pass out. Again, Amos was kept overnight for observation.

Emanuel had a good lecture about some of his games he played. This could have caused a death. He would need to be more careful.

In the past three years, the Millers had increased a lot of things on the farm. Then George Yoder informed them that he had sold the farm. The Millers would need to seek another location. The twins weren't too happy about moving because that meant going to a different school and making new friends.

The next month was a busy one. They would rent the Jake Gingerich farm. So there was a lot of packing to do. A truck was hired to move the livestock.

Neighbors came in to lend their helping hands. An assembly line was formed from the basement to a waiting wagon outside. About a six inch layer of oats was scooped into the bottom of the wagon. Then the jars of canned food were placed in the wagon, leaving some space between them. Another layer of oats was put on top of the jars. Then another layer of jars until the wagon was filled. At the new place, the jars were unloaded with the assembly line going in reverse order. Three wagons were needed to haul all the canned goods and boxes of dishes.

One of the hardest jobs of moving was loading the hay and corn into the wagons. The hay wasn't baled then like it is now. It was put in the barn by hand—loose.

Unloading the hay was easier. A harpoon was used which was attached to a rope that went to a carrier on a track located at the peak of the barn. A team of horses was hitched up to the long end of the rope. The harpoon was fastened to the hay on the wagon. On command, the horses would pull the rope which lifted the hay to the mow.

A big dinner would be brought in by the kind neighbors for events like this. After dinner, the ladies helped Susan unpack dishes and other items from boxes and place the things on shelves and in drawers. It would take Susan a few weeks to get organized.

It was a challenge with the livestock to get each cow trained to know which stanchion was hers at the new place. The horses were easier to train.

The twins found it adventurous to go to the woods and also to check out all the outbuildings. This house was much larger than they had before, so the twins had their own bedroom. More adjustments and changes were made.

What lay ahead for the Millers?

**Jake Gingerich Farm**

Chapter 7

# New School Adjustments

After moving day on Saturday to the Gingerich farm, Monday was upon them before they were ready. This was their first day of school, so Susan decided she would take the boys. She would take them to meet the new teacher.

The boys walked the two miles home after school. Amos thought those two miles would never end! The next morning, they would need to walk to school, so they would start earlier. Chores before going to school had to be done. The twins would wash the breakfast dishes for their mother.

In winter months, outside chores were also done before heading out for school in sometimes zero weather. Susan would wrap scarves around their necks and faces with only their mouths and noses exposed. Only if the temperature dropped below zero did they get a ride in the buggy.

Triumph School was a one-room schoolhouse for all eight grades. The teacher would have the seventh and eighth graders help out with the younger students. It was also the older grades duty to take turns to go to school early to start the wood fire in the furnace. It would usually be warm in the schoolhouse by the time the others got there. When their class work was completed, the boys would go out and split wood. The lunch buckets were placed outside in the snow to keep cold during the winter months.

The boys soon discovered a shortcut to school through the fields and woods. If the snow was too deep, they had to take the route by road. On their way home from school, they would pick up their mail, which was three-quarter mile from home.

During the summer, the boys would take turns riding their horse, Lester, to fetch the mail. Lester was a smaller horse, so it was easier to get on and off. The boys had him trained to lower himself so it made it even easier to get on his back. They would say, "Stretch Lester," and he would stretch his front feet out in front of him. Sometimes after getting the mail, Lester was in a hurry to get back home and didn't obey the stretching command.

Ezra felt ornery and sometimes would get ahead of the other boys on their way home from school. He would catch a ride with a neighbor. The neighbor would ask, "Shall we wait for the twins?"

"Naw, that's okay, just go on," Ezra would answer. So Ezra was the first one home on more than one occasion.

One day Amos complained to his mother, "Mom, Ezra just tells the neighbor to go on and not wait for us."

Susan then had a talk with Ezra telling him if he doesn't share the ride with his brothers, then he doesn't need a ride either. After that the twins rode whenever the neighbor offered a ride to Ezra.

Sometimes Ezra would stay after school and carry wood for the next morning. The teacher would then offer him a ride home. On their way, they would pass the twins. The teacher would then drop Ezra off about three-quarter mile from home.

Now the twins would get upset that they weren't being offered a ride.

"Guess what?" Ezra told the boys, "The teacher lets me drive sometimes."

"Well, if you don't stop and give us a ride, we'll tell Mom."

The next evening, Ezra passed the twins. He was driving the teacher's car again. He never stopped to give them a ride which upset the twins terribly.

"Mom," Amos said as soon as he got home, "Ezra drives the teacher's car sometimes."

"Are you sure?" she asked in astonishment.

"Yes, Mom, we saw him," answered Amos.

That evening Susan let her husband deal with Ezra!

The second year they attended Triumph School, Ezra graduated. After that Ezra would take the twins to school by horse and buggy although he tried to get out of it.

The teacher quite often asked Amos to help the other students (mostly the girls) with their fractions. Amos enjoyed this as arithmetic was his favorite subject. He especially liked to help Martha Bontrager. He had a crush on her. (He found out later, she had a crush on him too.)

It was their second Christmas at Triumph School. The teacher asked Amos, "Would you play Santa for us this year?"

"Sure, if you get me a Santa suit," came Amos's reply.

The other children in the school didn't know about the plan. The mothers had been invited for the Christmas party. After the program, "Santa" arrived to pass out gifts from under the pine tree. Santa waited outside for the right time to go in. He knocked on the door, and the teacher said, "Now who could that be?" Going to the door she opened it, inviting Santa in. He came in with a "Ho, ho, ho!"

"Has everyone been good this year?" Santa asked.

"Yes!" came the chorus of voices.

Santa then called out all the names on the packages. A few of the other children helped Santa hand out the packages. Now Santa had stuffed a couple of pillows inside his suit. The suit, much too big, made it difficult to see and read all the names clearly. Coming to a gift for Martha's mother, Santa looked up to find her but couldn't spot her, so he called out, "Where's Johnny Polly?"

The children found this very funny. Amos had to hear about this in years to come. "Where's Johnny Polly?" "Where's Johnny Polly?"

Most of the children were surprised when Amos climbed out of the Santa suit. They thought this had been "a real Santa"!

✧ ✧ ✧

The school had no running water, therefore a pump was on the outside, and all water was pumped by hand. Outside toilets furnished room for Mother Nature's calls. Electric lights were provided for the school. These were some good memories of my days at Triumph School.

**Triumph School**

Chapter 8

# Rabbit Hunt — Coon Fight

"Look! Fresh snow on the ground," came Amos's excited voice when he got up on Thanksgiving morning. The twins were quite excited about the six inches of fresh snow that covered the ground. This was ideal for rabbit hunting with the family dog, Maggie. Maggie wasn't just a good livestock dog, but was also a good hunting dog—if you left your gun at home. She was gun shy and would hide if she saw you had a gun.

Starting along the road ditch, Amos and Andy saw a rabbit dart out. The boys had Maggie trained quite well. Maggie chased the rabbit and caught it. Then she held it down with her front paws until the twins could catch up. Letting go, Maggie jumped up and down, excited about her first catch of the day.

The rabbit was taken to their father to dress out. The twins returned to their hunting with Maggie close to their heels. Sometimes Maggie got so excited she'd shake a rabbit as the twins would holler out, "No, Maggie!" She would then hold the rabbit with her front paws until Amos or Andy arrived. John was surprised when his sons brought home six more rabbits.

The twins were cold by now so they went into the house to warm up before they started on their next round of hunting.

Maggie soon had two more rabbits chased near the trees by the barn. One of the rabbits ran under a pile of lumber. Andy poked a stick at one end while Amos went to the other end. Sure enough, the rabbit ran straight into Amos's hands. They returned to the house with two more rabbits.

By noon, nine more rabbits were caught. What an excited dog—and boys! Now John informed the twins this was enough rabbits for one day.

When Susan called the boys for dinner, they didn't need to be called twice. They had worked up quite an appetite.

A neighbor boy, Johnny Buzinski, had gone rabbit hunting that day too, but had come home empty-handed. He couldn't believe it when the twins told him later of their day's catch. It was hard on him that the boys had outdone him in rabbit hunting.

✧ ✧ ✧

In February 1997, I had the opportunity to meet Johnny Buzinski again. This was the first time Johnny and I had seen each other since we were ten years old.

During that visit, I had to bring up the rabbit hunting experience we had forty-seven years ago. Johnny said, "You had to remember that event."

Now it was Johnny's turn to bring up another event that took place back then. Johnny used to come down to our place and wait till we were done with our chores, then he would go with us back to the river to swim.

I'm glad Johnny reminded me of this event while we were visiting. He helped recall the story as it took place back then.

✧ ✧ ✧

The lane we walked on going back to the river had some sandy spots which would have some sandburs in them. Andy went barefooted more than Amos did, so he could run right through the sandburs without them sticking to his feet.

Amos's feet were softer so the sandburs would stick to his feet. He had to stop and pick them off.

Johnny made the remark, "Why don't the sandburs stick to Andy's feet?" Amos thought he had to answer Johnny, so he said, "Andy's feet are gwaned to it." Now the twins didn't know all the English words yet. They and the other Amish families spoke Pennsylvania Dutch to each other. They referred to people who were not Amish as English.

Johnny looked at Amos and asked, "What does 'gwaned to it' mean?" Emanuel replied, "It means used to it." Amos had to hear for quite a few years about being "gwaned to it."

## Raccoon Fight

It had been quite cold in December 1949, but the zero weather didn't keep the twins and Maggie from venturing out into the woods to see what kind of animals they could chase up.

One in-between Sunday forenoon, the twins were out in the woods on one of those ventures, to find what they could chase up.

Maggie started to bark and chased a raccoon up a tree. Now the twins should've continued on, but it was too tempting. They couldn't let that coon just sit up there. So they started to throw sticks up the tree to make the coon come down. The coon finally got tired of those sticks, and down he came. He ran for the river with Maggie not too far behind him.

The river had some thin ice spots. They held the coon, but Maggie broke down through the ice and started to swim in the cold icy water after the coon. The twins urged Maggie on, so she would keep swimming to get the coon. When she got close enough, she would bite his tail and he would turn around to bite Maggie. Finally, Maggie got the coon off the ice and into the water. Now is when the fight really began! Maggie was under water, then the coon was on the bottom. The boys saw Maggie was starting to bleed, so they called her to come back, but she kept on going till the coon got away.

Maggie found out, as did the twins, that this was a lot different than catching rabbits. When Maggie came out on the river bank, she was cold and bleeding. She just lay down for a while—she was quite exhausted!

The twins were quite worried by now, not sure if Maggie would make it or not. After a while they got her up and started back home. They were concerned what Dad would say when he saw what shape Maggie was in.

They took Maggie into the barn when they got home and started to dry her off. She started to bleed more as the ice thawed off her hair and off the cuts she had. They decided they better go to the house and tell Dad what happened. He would check Maggie out.

John found several large cuts where the coon cut her up pretty bad. John helped his sons clean Maggie's cuts and dress them. He said she would probably be okay in a few days.

Dad let them know, "Under no circumstance should you let Maggie get involved with a raccoon in the water." They did tell him that they called Maggie back but she just kept on going.

John said, "You should have left the coon up the tree and this would not have happened."

It was a few days before Maggie started to move around and be herself again.

Chapter 9

# An Adventure – Sly Fox

It was a beautiful summer day. The sun was shining, casting its bright rays on the lush green lawn and fields.

"Can we go outside and play?" Amos asked his mother.

"Well, I wish you'd wash the dishes first," came the answer.

"Aw, Mom, why can't we play first?"

"If you don't want to eat, then I guess you don't need to wash dishes."

"Okay! That's a deal!" and the twins were off.

After a while, Susan went to the garden to bring in some fresh vegetables. She said to the twins who were nearby, "Now boys, just because you don't eat doesn't mean you can play all day! I want you to go across the road and hoe those potatoes and sweet corn."

This was more than the twins bargained for. They had thought if they didn't eat, they could play all day. There were twelve rows altogether. The patch was next to a clover field which was in full bloom and smelled really good.

The sun was quite warm and the boys had worked up an appetite. The twins had slowed down in their hoeing, because by now their energy level was getting pretty low.

"I'm getting pretty hungry, Amos," Andy said.

"I'm hungry too," Amos admitted. "But I'm not ready to wash those dishes!"

"Me either."

"I know what Andy!" Amos had come up with an idea. "Why don't we eat some of those clover blooms. They sure smell sweet."

"Hey, I never thought of that," Andy answered. So the boys ate clover blooms and drank lots of water, but that didn't take care of their hunger pains.

Reaching down to pinch more clover blooms, Amos saw a big black snake. Screaming "Snake!" the twins ran for the house, sure the snake was coming after them.

Coming inside the house, they were both out of breath when Susan asked her sons, "Are you done already?"

"No . . . , because . . . a snake . . . chased us out!"

"Well, I'll get your dad to go with you and kill the snake," said Susan. Now the twins knew they weren't excused from their work yet.

Later Amos couldn't keep quiet about how hungry they had been. "Mom, we were so hungry that's why we ate the clover blooms."

"Now remember boys, I said if you don't eat, then you won't have to wash dishes, but you ate the clover blooms, so now you can wash the dinner dishes."

Maybe the snake was like Satan trying to get you to do things . . . thinking nobody will know.

After the dishes were done, the twins were sent out to do more hoeing. "Why don't we wait until Mom and Dad go chore and then we can sneak some crackers? Mom won't notice if a few crackers are gone," said Amos to Andy.

So that is what they did. Getting back to the patch the boys emptied their pockets of soda crackers and began munching away. They both felt better and went back to hoeing. After the hoeing was finished, they headed for the house.

"Did you do your chores?" Susan asked the boys.

"No, not yet," they answered.

"Then get to it."

By now it seemed they had done a lot of work for one day. Coming in from doing her chores, Susan told the twins, "You can help me with supper. Amos you set the table, and Andy can help me fix supper. Now remember, we'll need two less plates tonight because you two aren't eating."

The boys obeyed their mother. As Amos was setting the plates, his stomach was growling.

"Who has been in the soda crackers?" came Susan's voice from the pantry.

Startled the boys looked at each other in amazement. "Why did Mother have to make soup tonight?" thought Amos.

"Boys, have you been sneaking crackers today?"

They looked at each other, not saying a word. Susan could tell by their guilty looks that they had eaten the crackers.

"I guess there won't be any supper for you two tonight now," Susan said in disappointment. "Maybe you'll know how to listen and obey after this. Now anytime you want to start eating tomorrow you can, but the dishes will need to be done too."

"You know boys, there are a lot of people going hungry, and so you shouldn't complain when there are dishes to be done. Just be thankful for the food God has provided for us." The boys were glad to wash the dishes from there on without complaining. They had learned a lesson.

Through this experience, the twins also learned there was no need to try to keep things from their mother. She would find out sooner or later. The lesson Susan taught her sons lasted a lot longer than any spanking would have. They were thankful for a loving, caring mother.

Another year went by and the twins were eleven years old. Emanuel had begun working out for other people, making the twins work more at home. Amos and Andy had to milk two cows each. Amos also fed the fryers and Andy helped feed the pigs and other livestock. All these chores didn't excuse the twins from dishes and other chores around the house.

During this time, Susan's father, Grandpa Emanuel Bontrager, stayed with them. Susan's brothers and sisters took turns having their father for three months at a time. This was extra work for Susan, but she was glad for the opportunity to care for her father.

The twins felt very grown up around Grandpa Bontrager because he was such a short fellow. The twins were already taller than their grandpa! Grandpa was a man of few words, who read a lot. He would often pull out his pocket watch and show the boys what time it was. Susan would sew new pants and shirts for her dad and also mend his old clothes.

The twins would start the motor at the windmill to run the pump jack. The pump jack had an open gear. Sometimes the boys would gather some tall weeds to put into the gear and watch them get crushed up. One day, Amos didn't get his fingers away in time, and the grass pulled his fingers into the gear. It stalled the motor and Amos had to reverse the gears to get his fingers free. This was a very painful ordeal.

Amos didn't get too much sympathy. His father reminded him that he was old enough to know better than to poke those weeds into the gears. He soaked Amos's fingers in kerosene for the pain and then bandaged them up with salve. About three weeks later, Amos lost the nails on those fingers. Amos was too active which got him into trouble too often. Susan always said, "Amos was always the leader."

Amos used the Radio Flyer wagon to haul feed for the fryers which were located in a small brooder house in the orchard. Amos played with the Radio Flyer a lot too. He would pretend the wagon was a truck. His voice played the motor of his make-believe truck and that got him into trouble. Often his father would call, "Amos"—but he couldn't hear because his motor was too loud.

In the winter months, Amos would pull the piano chair to the window and pretend to be driving a truck. But when the motor got too loud, Susan would need to remind him to be quiet. Why was he always the one to get into trouble?

Susan was having some health problems. John would take her to the doctor quite often. The twins were real concerned about their mother, so they put in extra effort in helping around the house.

"Boys," said John one day, "your mother will need to go to the hospital for an operation soon."

Now Amos was worried. Would his mother come home alive? "Dad," he asked, "will she come back home okay?"

"Now Amos," John assured his son, "your mom will be in the hospital about a week and yes, we're sure she's going to be fine."

Amos felt better knowing this. A few days later, Susan told her sons, "We're having a hired girl, Lizzie Mast, to come in while I'm at the hospital. And boys, you mind Lizzie just as if she were your mother."

Lizzie came a few days before Susan left for the hospital. "Lizzie, I want you to know the twins are good dishwashers," Susan explained to her maid.

It didn't take long for the twins to be comfortable around Lizzie. But everyone was glad to have Susan return from the hospital. It seemed like a long time to Amos that his mother had gone, but she was back now, so that's all that mattered.

Lizzie ended up staying at the Millers for most of the summer. The twins got used to having Lizzie around, like a big sister they never had.

Emanuel had a few dates with Lizzie which excited Amos. Amos was hoping they would even get married some day, but things didn't turn out that way. Amos felt sad when he found out they quit dating. But what did an eleven-year-old boy know about dating? He just knew Lizzie was a wonderful girl to have around. Why couldn't they get together?

## Sly Fox

John was trying hard to increase their income in order to pay for Susan's operation. He got in touch with a feed company salesman about raising turkeys. After discussing a plan at length, John informed his family. They would be raising turkeys.

Soon the field man was there informing them what was needed to start the business. The chicken house needed to be remodeled. Lots of feeders would need to be purchased including water fountains. Heated brooders were needed so the little turkey chicks could stay warm.

The day finally arrived that the chicks came. What a chirping sound! The slightest little commotion would make them pile into the corners, frightened. Sometimes the boys would take turns staying with the chicks at night. John began to understand why not many people raised turkeys.

At ten weeks old, the turkeys were moved out on the range. Range shelters had to be built along with roosting shelves. A fence was also built. Shortly after putting the turkeys on range, dead turkeys were found every morning.

The boys took turns staying out at night to see what was going on. So one night after hearing a great commotion, they discovered a sly old fox close by. This was what frightened the turkeys and made them pile together. Some were smothered to death. After that, they pulled the double buggy down to the range and one of the boys would sleep in the buggy. Now this was scary business for the twins, so when it was their turn, they would get Ezra to sleep in the buggy too.

"I don't think anyone would need to sleep in the buggy anymore," said John. "Just having the buggy there, the fox would probably think somebody is in it."

So it was decided the boys would sleep in their own beds. The sly old fox was smarter than they thought and came out again that night. Needless to say, every night after that, someone slept in the buggy until the turkeys were sold. They couldn't afford to lose more turkeys. The prices were down when the time came to sell the turkeys, but they had learned a lot by now.

The following year, they raised another batch of turkeys, but then John decided that was it. The prices at selling time were a little better, but John felt the risk was too high. Sometimes when it rained, the turkeys would turn their heads toward the sky and drown themselves. This had been a good experience for the Millers, but no more turkeys for them!

Chapter 10

# An Attempted Kidnapping

Susan was scurrying about the kitchen trying to get everything in order and breakfast on the table while John and the boys were doing chores. A door slammed and she knew they were coming so she poured the tomato gravy into a bowl. The fried mush was in the warmer and ready to be set on the table.

After everyone was seated and prayers said, Susan looked at John with a sigh. "Do you suppose I could go into town this morning, John?"

"Well, I don't know why not," came the answer. "Amos, you can hitch up and take Mom into town," John said looking at his son.

"Oh, sure Dad, I'd like that."

After breakfast Amos helped his Mother with the dishes, and then asked, "Are you ready, Mom?"

"Yes, Amos, you can hitch up the horse. I'll be right out."

Amos was smacking his lips already. He loved to go shopping with Mother because she usually stopped at the Dairy Queen for an ice cream cone on the way home.

They stopped at the feed store, and then went to the grocery store in Oelwein. After tying the horse to the hitch rail, Amos told his mother, "I'm going to use the restroom at the gas station. I'll be right back. I'll meet you in the store."

"Okay, Amos, that's fine," said Susan.

When Amos entered the restroom, he noticed another man in there.

"Hi there!" the man had said.

"Hi," came Amos's voice.

"How are you, young man?"

"I'm fine," answered Amos.

"You have fine wide shoulders, young man. Just right to be a football player!"

Amos was beginning to get uneasy with this stranger.

"You know, you're just the guy I need to play football. How old are you?"

"Er-r-r, em-m-m. . . ," Amos cleared his throat for by now he was getting nervous. "I'm eleven."

"I've never had a son of my own. How would you like to go home with me? I could put you through school. Your parents wouldn't know what happened to you. I'd love to have you for my boy."

Amos was getting pretty scared by now. He noticed the man was lurking at the doorway. Amos kept wondering how he would get out . . . Was this strange man going to kidnap him? Surely not! . . . What if he never saw his family again? Chills crept up and down his spine . . . Surely by now, Mother would wonder where he was or what took him so long . . . What should he do? How could he escape this guy? . . .

Amos took a few steps backwards. The man moved a few steps closer to Amos. By now Amos's heart was beating hard. Each time Amos took a step back, the man took a step forward.

The man reached out to grab Amos. Amos made a duck under his arm. Amos ran for the door, but the man grabbed Amos's arm and pulled him back. Terrified, Amos tore loose from the man and ran out the door toward the grocery store!

Standing inside the grocery store door, Amos took time to try to settle his throbbing heart before he found his mother. He was so glad to see other people around. He was sure the man wouldn't follow him now. What if this guy was waiting on the outside when they got out? Amos went in search of his mother.

Amos didn't want his mother to be frightened, so he said nothing of the kidnap attempt. His mom didn't ask any questions and was soon ready to go.

As Amos untied the horse, his knees were shaking. He made a quick dash for the buggy and slapped the horse's rump with the reins. The horse took off at once.

"Are you in a hurry?" asked Susan, looking at Amos.

"Yeah, kind of," came her son's reply. As they turned in at the Dairy Queen, Amos relaxed a bit. He would just as soon go on home, but he didn't dare say so to Mother.

As the evening wore on, Amos began to relax more and more. He felt safer being at home now.

For several days, Amos just couldn't get the experience out of his mind. What if the man had kidnapped him? Where would he be right now? He didn't tell anyone of his ordeal. He didn't want his parents to worry about it. Amos always felt the Lord had protected him.

✧ ✧ ✧

The Revealing

In the past years, it's been hard to keep this experience to myself. Whenever I would hear of a kidnaping, memories of my own experience would make chills go up and down my spine. I know my life would have been different had this guy succeeded in getting me back then.

This was one of the hardest chapters to write in this whole book. The memories came back and my tears flowed as I wrote about my experience. I know now that I should have shared this with my parents and family back then.

On June 21, 1997, I went to Vermontville, Michigan to visit with my dad. He had prostate cancer and been growing weaker the past two weeks. He was eighty-seven in January that year.

While I was visiting with him, I shared with him the experience that I had gone through. I asked Dad to forgive me for not telling him years ago. Dad forgave me. We cried in happiness as we shared with each other. After sharing this with Dad, a heavy burden was lifted from my heart. I would advise anyone who goes through a traumatic experience to share it with parents and family while you still can—before it's too late.

Our Dad passed away July 10, 1997. Now we have no living parents. I would advise the younger generation to love your parents while you still have the opportunity. The time that we had our parents to love seems so short.

✧ ✧ ✧

Threshing season arrived. This would be Amos and Andy's first experience at threshing. When the oats and wheat turned to a nice golden color, it was ready to be cut with a binder which would put the stalks of grain into bundles. These bundles would then be put into shocks to cure and dry out until threshing time.

Many times shocks were made by moonlight because it would be cooler at night. Most of the shocks contained ten to twelve bundles. The bundles would be set on end, leaning them together at the top. Then one bundle was spread out on top to keep the rain off.

The boys would try hard to keep up with their dad on the binder. But John was usually about three rounds ahead of them. A crock jug was used to keep the oil in for the binder. Another crock jug was used for drinking water. The jugs were placed near the shocks to keep cool.

One day Amos needed a drink and tipped the wrong jug. To his surprise he got a mouthful of oil! After spitting and much wiping, Amos wasn't too happy about the incident. Ezra had moved the water jug and hadn't told the others. Amos blamed Ezra for moving the jug on purpose. The others laughed at Amos's mistake, but Amos didn't find it funny at all.

Usually about six weeks after the grain was in shocks, the neighbors would get together to thresh the oats or wheat. About twenty farmers in the area would help each other. One farmer owned the threshing machine and a big power unit to run the machine. This farmer charged the others three cents per bushel for the use of the machine.

There were usually twelve hay wagons to haul the bundles to the threshing machine. About eight men would be the "pitchers." They would pitch the bundles onto the wagon with a guy on the wagon arranging the bundles until he had a load. The wagon was then taken to the threshing machine to unload.

On some days, the temperatures got up to 120 degrees. On one particular threshing day, some of the men got overheated and needed to sit under the shade tree for a while. Not Amos! He kept right on going!

"I'm pretty proud of you, Amos," John told him that evening, "You outworked some of the men."

One day, the threshing crew was short of help, so Amos decided he could load by himself. He would pitch a batch of bundles onto the wagon, then jump up on the wagon and arrange them, get back down, pitch up more bundles, climb up on the wagon and arrange—until he had done six loads that day. Talk about a tired twelve-year-old boy that night!

When threshing season was over, everyone would get together for homemade ice cream. Everyone would fill a freezer and bring along cake and chips to help celebrate the harvest. The young boys would play softball.

What a rewarding and enjoyable evening they always had!

Chapter 11

# Moving Again — Working Out

The spring of 1951 brought another adjustment for the Millers. They would be moving to the Dan Bontrager farm. The twins weren't too excited about moving and adjusting to a different school again. "Now Amos, you boys will adjust to the school, and you'll like it a lot," Susan assured her son.

The farm was smaller and there would be less chores to do, but that didn't mean more time to play, because now the twins would have more time to help their mother.

Because the Bontrager farm was smaller, some of the livestock needed to be sold. It was hard to see some of the cows being shipped off as the twins had become quite attached to them. Six cows were sold plus some of the other livestock. That money helped the Millers meet the expenses of moving.

This move took longer because they had twelve miles to go. The week after the family moved, they made several trips to get all the hay and grain.

The house was smaller with only two bedrooms upstairs. The first bedroom was at the top of the stairs. You needed to go through that room to get to the second bedroom. Ezra was older so he got the back room, leaving the larger hall bedroom for the twins, Johnny and Joni. Emanuel slept in the back bedroom when he was at home. He was working out during that time.

After a few weeks, everyone adjusted to their new location. One day John remarked, "You know it would be nice if we could just buy this place." He felt it was hard on the family to be moving all the time.

On Monday morning, the twins got up early and prepared for school which was at the end of their three-quarter mile lane. Susan walked the boys to school. They met the teacher and the rest of the students and signed in for that year.

At noon the boys would run home for lunch and then run back to school. Lots of times, the noon dishes were still to be washed at night when the boys got home from school as Susan was too busy to get that done yet. So the boys didn't hurry home as dishwashing wasn't one of their favorite chores.

The new school was okay until Amos wasn't getting all A's anymore. He was having trouble reading. He kept reading the same line over and over until he started using his finger to guide him.

"Mom," Amos said one night while he was helping his mother in the kitchen, "I'm having trouble reading at school."

Looking up, Susan asked, "What seems to be the problem?"

"I keep reading the same lines over and over. It seems I can't remember what I just read."

"I'll talk to your dad about it Amos, maybe we need to take you to an eye doctor."

That night after supper, Susan confronted John with Amos's problem. "John, Amos says he's having trouble with his reading at school."

"What kind of trouble?" John asked.

Susan related what Amos had told her.

"Well, it probably wouldn't hurt to get him to an eye doctor," John said.

The next week found Amos in the doctor's office for an eye examination.

After the exam the doctor said, "Mrs. Miller, your son definitely needs glasses. I can understand why he would have trouble at school. The eyes play an important role in learning. With the help of glasses, I think this can be corrected. Also he needs to do some exercises at home and needs to wear an eye patch for three months."

With the new glasses and exercises, Amos soon brought his grades back up.

Andy was doing okay in school with his studies, but was having trouble getting along with some of the boys. One afternoon he got into a fight with one of them after school. Both boys had some adjustments to make.

The twins were glad when the school year passed and summer was around the corner.

Sometimes Amos felt as though his mother was trying to make girls out of them. He would put on an apron when helping Mother with the baking. Andy would rather clean house.

Susan enjoyed and appreciated her sons' help. She often wondered why she didn't have daughters. What would it be like to have a daughter helping her all the time? But she shouldn't question the Lord's plans for her. The boys were good at helping out, and she was thankful for that!

Several times their Sunday company would marvel at the delicious cake or pies. Then Susan would say, "You need to give Amos the credit for that!"

Amos would feel ashamed—what would they think of this boy doing the baking? Mother would say, "Amos, it's nothing to be ashamed of. I'm proud of you that you can help me and bake like that."

Another job the twins had was going to the pump to fill the water buckets since none of the houses they lived in had running water. They kept saying, "I did it the last time." Then the other one would say, "No, I did it last." So Mother would say, "Okay, you can both go!" So both boys ended up carrying the same bucket. When they got into the house, Mother would say, "Now, that wasn't so bad after all, was it?" The boys would look at each other with a smirk.

Susan thought it very important that her sons brush their teeth every day, so she made a chart. "Now boys," she said, showing the chart she had created, "every day that you brush your teeth, you put a check mark here. Then at the end of the week if you have checked each day, I will give you a penny."

"Wow!" The boys said. They couldn't believe their good fortune—just for brushing their teeth! Very seldom did they forget to brush their teeth.

John had decided they needed more income. They would try raising capons. They had to get the chicken house all cleaned up and in shape. After several weeks of cleaning, one day 2,000 baby chicks arrived. They made more chores for the twins. Feeding and watering 2,000 chicks kept them busy!

At three-weeks old, the chicks needed to be caponized. They needed to be watched real close after that in case of swelling. Some of the chicks swelled to the size of baseballs. Then a needle had to be injected to release the pressure. The other chicks would sometimes pick on the swelled ones and nearly kill them. A mixture of tar and turpentine was mixed and put on the swelling. When the chicks started to pick, it wouldn't taste so good! They would run to the water fountain, shaking their heads. This was better than raising those turkeys in the past.

The following year, they raised mallard ducks too. The twins enjoyed the ducks more. The drakes had such colorful feathers. Amos enjoyed finding the ducks' nests, usually next to the hayfield. The boys also enjoyed watching the hens waddle along with their little ones behind them—up to twenty little ducklings. Sometimes the boys would catch a duckling only to be attacked by the drakes. At the end of that year, they had about 150 ducklings.

The dozen guineas they had helped to keep foxes away. The guineas sure made a shrill cry if something unusual went on. A few colorful banties *[bantams]* were seen on the farm too. Most of them went to roost on the lower tree branches and some in the cow barn.

This was surely a change from what the twins were used to.

## Working Out

With the small farm there wasn't enough work to keep thirteen-year-old Amos and Andy busy. When Steve Yoder came to see John about a hired hand, it was decided Amos would work out. He would be the one to go help Steve.

"I need somebody to work the fields for me," said Steve to John.

Turning to Amos, John asked, "Do you think you could handle that?"

"I could try," came Amos's answer, unsure if he really would be able to do that. He wanted to help Mom and Dad with expenses.

"Would $15 a week be okay?" asked Steve.

"That sounds reasonable," answered John.

Amos felt a little nervous about the deal. It wasn't like working for his dad.

Steve's farm was about six miles from the Miller's farm which seemed like a long way to Amos. When they arrived, Steve took Amos to the barn.

"Now here are the two horses you'll be using and there are their harnesses. I'll let you harness them while I get the plow ready."

When Amos saw the large Belgian horses, he had some doubts as to whether he could get those heavy harnesses on them. The horses were about twenty inches taller than Amos and the harnesses hung as high as Amos's head.

"Now what?" thought Amos. He needed to figure this one out. His dad always harnessed up the horses at home.

Not wanting to tell Steve he couldn't harness up the horses, Amos looked around the barn for something to stand on. Finding a five-gallon bucket, he turned it upside down.

Standing on the bucket, he pulled at a harness. Kerplop! Down came the harness—and Amos. Gathering himself up off the floor, Amos moved the bucket to one of the horses. Then he drug the harness over to the bucket. He managed to lift the front part of the harness on the horse, then the back part.

Steve came in to see what was taking so long. He soon had the other horses harnessed and helped hitch them to the plow.

Steve went along to the field to get Amos started, then returned to the buildings. Amos was on his own!

The forenoon seemed to drag on forever. Amos thought dinnertime would never come. How he wished he had a whip to keep those outside horses going faster. The horses knew there was a different voice behind them. Amos was so hoarse by noon, he could hardly talk. The horses probably thought he didn't sound too threatening.

Amos adjusted some, and the work went more smoothly. He would plow every night until eight o'clock. He had tiring days and was glad to go up to the house, eat a good supper, and go to bed.

By Wednesday, Amos was so homesick, he was beside himself. This was Amos's first experience away from home. By

Friday night, Amos could hardly wait until supper was over so Steve could take him home.

"It's so good to be home, Mom. I was so homesick this week," said Amos. This was one of the longest weeks of Amos's life.

Now Amos wasn't looking forward to Monday morning. But Steve was there bright and early to pick him up. The second week went better, but Amos was glad to see Friday night come again so he could be back home with his own family.

Amos confided to his dad about how much work he had to do. John had a talk with Steve on Monday morning about the deal. Steve agreed to pay $20 a week from now on. Amos worked for six weeks for Steve.

Amos was so glad to be back home that he never complained when told to do something. He did work for Steve a few days a week after that when cultivating time came. He was thankful for a loving mom and dad and his brothers.

Bontrager School

Dan Bontrager Farm

Chapter 12

# Family Trials

Ezra worked out part-time to help with the family's expenses. When he was at home, he helped with the farming and chores.

On this particular day, it was rainy out so John and Susan decided to make a trip to town. "Dad, I could cut that lumber up while you're in town," said Ezra.

"No, Ezra, I'd rather you wait until I get back and I'll help you," came his father's advice.

John and Susan had just left when Ezra decided, "Now I might as well get to that lumber pile. I'll surprise Dad and have a lot done before he gets back home."

It wasn't long after he started the buzz saw that a board got stuck and pulled Ezra's hand into the saw. Ezra shut the motor off and took a quick look at the cut up fingers. He ran to get a container of kerosene—that would stop the bleeding. After some time soaking, it just wouldn't stop bleeding. He wrapped the fingers in some clean white rags and waited until his mom and dad got home.

The pain was so great by now. Why didn't he obey his father? How he wished he would have. But it was too late. He knew his father would be terribly upset.

After taking a look at the fingers, John said, "Looks like we'll need to get to a doctor, Ezra. I wish you would have listened to me and waited until I got home to cut up that lumber. Now see what happens when you don't listen?"

Yes, Ezra could see. He didn't say a word all the way to the doctor's office. They saved the fingers and sewed them up and back together, but the doctor informed them that Ezra would never have full use of those fingers. They would be deformed and the feeling would be gone to some extent. How sorry Ezra was he had disobeyed his father and not taken advice. He would need to do better from now on.

Ezra had been hanging around with a rowdy bunch Sunday evenings at the Singing. John and Susan talked to him a lot about keeping away from them. One night Ezra decided to pack up and leave. He was tired of this nagging and complaining all the time. Ezra waited until everyone was sound asleep and quietly slipped out with his belongings.

The next morning John got up and called, "Ezra" from the stairway door. There was no answer. Again he called, "Ezra." Finally he called out, "Amos."

"Yeah?" came the sleepy boy's voice.

"Get up to do chores and wake Ezra."

The twins got dressed, then made their way down the stairs.

"Where's Ezra? Why didn't you wake him?" asked John.

"He's not in his room," answered Amos.

"What?" came the shocked voice of Susan.

"No, Mom and Dad, he's not there."

Susan's tears fell unchecked down her face as she said, "Oh, where have we failed? . . . John, go out and see if Ezra isn't just outside somewhere."

John put his chore boots on and left the house. Checking the barn first, he found that Ezra's buggy and horse were still there. Returning to the house, he told the others, "The horse and buggy are still here, but Ezra's gone."

Susan cried as she went about preparing the morning meal.

After a quiet breakfast for which nobody had an appetite now, John and Susan decided to go talk to some of Ezra's friend's parents. Maybe his buddies would know of his whereabouts. No one seemed to know what happened to him. Ezra hadn't always given all his money home, so they were sure he had some money on him.

Two weeks passed and no word had been received as to Ezra's whereabouts. Always when it came to meals, Susan would tell the boys, "Set a plate for Ezra too, maybe that will make him homesick enough so he'll want to come home." So they would always set a plate for Ezra. Mealtimes were always the most difficult to get through. Wouldn't it be better if they didn't need to look at that empty plate each time? But Susan always insisted, "Set a plate for Ezra."

Lots of tears were shed at this time. They missed Ezra a lot. If only they knew he was okay somewhere. Why did he leave? Had they been too harsh with him about being with his wild buddies? Every meal was spent in tears. When Susan called the boys to come for a meal, she would always call out Ezra's name too. Then the crying would start because Ezra didn't come.

Amos was getting tired of all the crying. Lots of times, he just sat there and wouldn't eat. "Amos, you need to eat something," Susan would say while wiping at her tears. So for Mother's sake, Amos would eat.

One day a letter arrived from relatives in Indiana stating they had seen Ezra there. John talked of going to Indiana to find his son and bring him home.

Amos was glad when Ezra did come back, and the ordeal was over now. Ezra didn't have too many dates, but had part in several weddings after that. Melvin Chupp asked him to have part with Barbara Miller, a sister to Melvin's future bride. Ezra agreed to have part with her in Melvin's wedding. He ended up asking her for a date.

The twins were being quite inquisitive about this gal, so they asked Ezra, "How big is she anyway? How does she look?"

They didn't need to wait too long to find out as the romance continued. Ezra brought his date home one weekend.

When Barbara came downstairs the next morning, the twins asked their mother, "Who's that little girl? We thought Ezra was bringing Barbara home."

"Well boys, you be nice to that little girl because this is Barbara!" Susan said with a smile.

What a surprise they had. Why, Barbara was no taller than the twins! They had fun after that teasing Ezra about "his little girl."

The year 1953 was bringing another adjustment to the Millers. It was moving time once again! One of Dan Bontrager's girls was getting married and wanted to move onto the farm which the Millers were renting. It seemed like every time they thought they were getting ahead, there was another adjustment ahead.

They would be moving to the Noah Gingerich farm which was twice as big as the Dan Bontrager farm they were on. The house was like a mansion compared to the house they lived in now. There were four rooms upstairs and two bedrooms downstairs. But this would mean more work for Susan.

The Gingerich farm had a nice dairy setup plus hog and chicken shelters. John bought sixteen milking cows and hogs and chickens. This meant lots of chores for the boys.

The twins turned fourteen and were able to help more on the farm. Amos was glad the Gingerich farm was large enough that he didn't need to work out. A few sheep were bought to graze in the orchard so that meant less mowing.

One nice summer day, the twins were hauling manure to one of the back fields. They needed to go through a small pasture field and through a creek to get to the back field. The family dog, Maggie, always went along to unload and would chase up ground gophers or rabbits.

Maggie stopped at a hole and started digging. The boys stopped to see what was going on. Maggie kept barking and digging. They checked things out, but couldn't find anything except two holes in the ground, so they continued on. On their way back, they stopped again because Maggie was still digging. They poked the fork handle into one end, and Maggie ran to the other end, when out came an animal.

"What is that thing?" Andy asked his brother in astonishment.

"I don't know, Andy, it's not a coon," came the reply from Amos. This animal had a flat head with a white ring around its neck. It got away from Maggie and went into another hole farther away.

"Why don't we go home and get a shovel and dig the thing out?" suggested Amos.

"Good idea!" said Andy.

Getting up to the buildings, Amos ran into the shed to get the shovel. Running back out, he was stopped in his tracks by a voice.

"Now, what are you up to?" asked John.

"You see Dad . . . er. . . .we. . . uh . . . have an animal in a hole back in the field that we want to get out," came Amos's answer.

"Now just what kind of an animal?"

"I'm not sure," then Amos went on to explain what the animal looked like.

"Amos, you boys let that animal be. That sounds like a badger and those things are dangerous. You boys get back to your manure hauling."

For Amos and Andy, the fun had ended then and there. Surely this animal wasn't that bad. Back to their hard labor, they went again.

John kept reminding the boys about Maggie being a wonderful dog. She was a small breed of Collie. She was just a part of the family now. She had raised a litter of pups for them. They would never forget how she had saved Amos's life back on the Duffy farm.

The summer was over and time for school to start again. The twins were looking forward to their last year in school. After graduation, they wouldn't need to think about moving and making adjustments in yet another school.

Things weren't all easy that last school year. The twins would get up at 4:30 each morning, milk four cows each, fix their own lunch, wash dishes, and walk over a mile to school.

There was a little free time in the evenings before it was chore time again. Chores included pitching down hay from the hay mow, before dark Dad had said, and more cows to milk.

There were times when the twins didn't get started as early as they should have and darkness was upon them before they realized it. After pitching hay down in the dark, they soon learned their lesson. It was almost impossible to get the job done in the dark. John would never allow them to take a lantern for risk of fires.

Graduation Day arrived and the twins were happy to be home. But . . . oh . . . the farm work was never ending. If they weren't fixing fence then there was plowing, seeding, cultivating, shocking oats, always milking, feeding, the list went on and on.

A neighbor, Emanuel Miller, was good to have around. He operated a harness shop. His daughter, Fannie, had gone to the same school as the twins. On occasion, Emanuel would come down and knock on the door, then announce, "There's somebody here!" He would tell his dog, "Quit barking before you run your battery down!" Or he would say, "Be quiet or I'll kick your lights out and use my battery to charge you up again!" Quite the Emanuel, Amos thought when he was around him.

One early morning as Amos headed out to do chores, he heard someone shouting, "Help!" Looking down toward Emanuel's place, Amos saw smoke rolling out of his shop.

Amos filled two five-gallon buckets with water and ran for Emanuel's. He was exhausted by the time he arrived on the scene. It was too late. The fire was beyond their control.

Emanuel stood there crying, tears rolling down his cheeks. "I'm losing everything!" he sobbed. How he wanted to go in and retrieve some of his belongings, but the others held him back. When the fire truck arrived, they helped to save the house and a shed.

The shop was gone! Amos felt so helpless, standing there unable to save Emanuel's shop. The oil from the harnesses made the fire spread so fast.

Emanuel had made the mistake of pouring gasoline instead of kerosene in his oil heating stove. This had caused an explosion and caught Emanuel's hair and clothes on fire. Luckily he had extinguished the flames on himself without much damage.

The neighbors came to help for several weeks after the fire. They dug through the debris trying to find salvageable items. Everyone was black with soot. A new shop was put up as was the custom in a barn-raising. It took Emanuel several months to find equipment to replace the old. Emanuel was never the same "cheery" man after this happened. He ended up having a breakdown.

The twins were really glad to have graduated from school. The next school year, the Amish started their own private schools and hired their own teachers.

✧ ✧ ✧

The following was taken from a local newspaper. The headlines were written because the Amish didn't meet state requirements for teaching in their private schools.

## YOUNGSTERS WEEP, FLEE

### Iowa Forces Amish Children to Attend Public School

Hazleton Iowa (UPI) The children ran as they saw the yellow bus approach. They ran out of two one-room Amish schools, past their Amish teachers, and into nearby cornfields. Some wept as they ran. Twenty-eight youngsters tried in this manner, Friday, to escape going to public schools. Their mothers stood on the school porch and sobbed. Startled officials, who had come to take them away, paced the edges of the fields, watching the small hats bob among the corn stalks. In the end, the Amish teachers who have only eighth grade educations, persuaded the youngsters to give up.

Friday, they attended a non-sectarian public school for the first time. The children's parents are of the stern Amish sect that does not believe in education past the eighth grade. Consequently, the Amish religious school did not meet Iowa requirements for accreditation.

A small number of the Amish sect have held out against attempts by school officials to make their youngsters attend the worldly public schools. Some Amish children in the area do attend these schools. Amish are strict persons. They use horse drawn buggies instead of cars. Kerosene instead of electricity, and have buttons instead of newfangled zippers on their clothing.

Amish parents have been fined for refusing to allow their children to attend public schools. In some cases, court action has been instituted to take the farmer's livestock as payment of the fine.

However, officials of Buchanan County and the Oelwein School District are not sure the enforced attendance on Friday is the answer. They said it was possible there would be more trouble when school resumes on Monday.

## HYMN SINGING AMISH CHILDREN WIN TRUCE

Hazleton Iowa (UPI) Little Amish children, succeeding where their parents failed, turned back the power of the state with a hymn and remained free today to attend their simple rustic country schools.

County school officials consented to a temporary moratorium on their efforts to force the children into public schools, their families consider to be "too worldly." After a schoolhouse showdown here in which the singing children thwarted county authorities, Governor Harold E. Hughes stepped into the three-year controversy Monday and announced the truce. It was the children themselves who made the day.

STOPPED BY HYMN

County school officials accompanied by a truancy officer and sheriff's deputies, pushed their way into a one-room Amish schoolhouse Monday in an attempt to haul the children off to public school.

A barrier of bearded stern-faced Amish men broke in the path of the county authorities. Then as the parents stood by sobbing, the authorities advanced on the children. The children screamed and started to chant the Sunday School hymn, "Jesus Loves Me."

THE AUTHORITIES RETREATED

In Des Moines, Hughes announced the moratorium and said it would last until Iowa officials can confer with officials of other states that have faced similar situations. "Somewhere in the confines of society there must be a reasonable solution to this situation," the Governor said.

✧ ✧ ✧

Are we as strong in our faith as these people were back then? We can have a strong faith today if we believe in the Lord, that He sent His only Son for our salvation. We must remember that religion doesn't get us to Heaven, nor does any church denomination. It is only between us and the Lord, only by living for Him can we get to Heaven. Religion and denomination will not earn our way to Heaven. How do we handle things that interfere with our faith? Let's keep seeking in the true Word.

It was awesome to be there and to experience that milestone. Let's remember the faith our forefathers had. Let this encourage us to carry on in our faith.

John Yoder School

Noah Gingerich Farm

Chapter 13

# Marriage — Prison

Emanuel's wedding day was nearing as John and Susan made plans to leave for Indiana. This was exciting for the twins for they hadn't seen some of their cousins in nine years.

John checked out costs of train fares for the family. It was more economical to travel by train. The twins had never had a train ride before, so they were excited about that too.

Susan sewed new clothes for everybody in the family. The next thing on the list was to find someone to do chores.

The day of departure arrived and excitement showed in the Millers. After arriving in Chicago, they needed to switch trains. Amos wondered how they would ever find the right train—there seemed to be dozens of trains. Susan encouraged them,"Hurry, so we won't miss our train."

John had made arrangements for someone to pick them up at the station in Elkhart. From there they went to Amos's grandparents, Urias Millers.

They spent a night at Amos's Uncle Emery's place. Their boys raised and sold rabbits. Amos thought, "These boys have it made. They get to keep the money they receive from selling the rabbits." They didn't have an opportunity like this at home.

They also stayed at Amos's Uncle Emanuel's one night. They had a large dairy where they milked lots of cows.

The next day, John and Susan took the boys to Topeka to meet Dr. Hilderbrand so he could see the twins he had delivered fourteen years ago. He was glad to see the boys, and thanked the Millers for coming.

The wedding was over, and all too soon it was time to head for home. The twins had such a good time and weren't ready to go back home. But it was time to go home and get to work!

## Prison

Emanuels moved to Iowa after they were married and worked on a farm for an English farmer. It was during that summer, Emanuel didn't receive his classification in the mail for 1-W service. Later he received the draft classification 1A—that classification meant he was eligible to serve in the armed forces. To some, it seemed as though the courts and the mailman had it in for the Amish. They claimed they had sent his form to him, but Emanuel never received it.

Too much time had lapsed by now, so it was too late to apply for CO classification. Emanuel had to go to court because he refused to go into the Army. They ended up sentencing him to a prison in Springfield, Missouri for three years.

After this took place, Emanuel's wife Mary moved in with the Millers as she would have no income with Emanuel in prison. Mary ended up buying some fryers for an income. Amos ended up helping Mary take care of the fryers. Mary did well with the fryers that summer. She also worked out, cleaning house for the English.

Three months went by before Mary was allowed to visit her husband. After returning from her first trip to visit Emanuel, Mary had broken down and cried saying, "They didn't even let me touch him, and I had to talk through a glass." This was a trying ordeal for Mary and Emanuel, and their family. Lots of tears had been shed through the ordeal.

Another young man named Melvin Chupp was also sentenced to the same prison for the same reason. His wife Edna was a sister to Ezra's girlfriend, Barbara. Ezra and Barbara had part in Melvin's wedding.

Ezra traveled with Mary to Springfield, Missouri occasionally. On one of those trips he hadn't returned with Mary. "Where is Ezra?" Susan asked Mary.

"He decided to stay in Jamesport," answered Mary, knowing that the family would be disappointed in his decision. Ezra worked for the Smith Brothers, farming. He didn't return to Iowa.

Susan wrote a letter for *The Budget* concerning Emanuel's prison term.

As parents of Emanuel and his wife, Mary, we have received so many letters regarding our son and husband of Mary, Emanuel Jay Miller, being in federal prison.

We thank the people for their sympathy shown. We thought we would write in The Budget in answer to some of the letters. We understand why some thought Emanuel refused to do hospital work, because it mentioned that in the daily paper. On the day of Emanuel' s trial, a soldier explained on the witness stand what the 1-A-O class is, that it would include hospital work, but that hospital work would have been in the Army hospital and not civilian work.

Melvin Chupp and Emanuel were classed as 1A and 1-A-O and had no chance to do civilian work, so the reason they are in federal prison at Springfield, Missouri is being they refused to be inducted into the armed forces. Romans 8:28 says, "And we know that all things work together for good to them that love God, to them who are the called according to his purpose." It must have been God' s will that they are there for some "purpose." It is hard to be separated from wife, parents, and church, but they still have a lot to be thankful for, for God can be with them anyway!

We were down to visit the boys on the Christmas holidays. We found them well and in a good mood. They did not complain of being there on the prison farm. They work on the prison farm six hours a day, such work as helping pull out hedge fence, crush stone, grind shelled corn by the freight car loads, etc. They have around 500 hogs there on the 442 acre farm. The boys help to brand the sows.

Mrs. John U. Miller

July 9, 1953, Susan copied the following from Ezra's CO questionnaire. This rule allowed the Amish to be exempt from joining the armed forces.

Law under the provision of section 2(J) of the universal military training and service act as amended, any person who claims exemption from combatant training and service in the armed forces of the United States because he is by reason of religious training and belief, conscientiously opposed to participation in war in any form and such claim is sustained by the local board, shall if he is inducted into the armed forces, be assigned to noncombatant service as defined by the President, or shall, if found to be conscientiously opposed to participation in such noncombatant service in lieu of induction be ordered by his local board, subject to regulation prescribed by the President, to perform for a period of twenty-four consecutive months such civilian work contributing to the maintenance of the national health, safety, or interest as the local board deems appropriate, and any such person who fails or neglects to obey such order of the local board shall be subject to imprisonment.

Emanuel and Melvin both served some time in a Des Moines jail awaiting their trial. The following is taken from newspaper articles written about their trials.

November 3, 1953. Trials were conducted for two days. Emanuel Miller and Melvin Chupp were both found guilty of the charges in the trials in which they served as their own lawyers.

Assisting in the selection of the jurors was Emanuel E. Schrock, an Amish bishop of near Independence. Amish families and relatives of the two registrants attended the trials at Des Moines.

Emanuel Miller was found guilty of refusal to be inducted into the armed forces as a noncombatant and Melvin Chupp was found guilty of refusal to be inducted into the armed forces as a combatant. In the trial against Chupp, his statement to the jury was that according to his religious beliefs, he cannot take selective services training. "Jesus never killed his enemies. He let the enemies kill him. Therefore, I am here to give myself up to the jury."

In Miller's trial, he told the jury that the Constitution of the United States guarantees freedom of religion and that his own belief was opposed to military service.

The two men were sentenced by Judge William Riley at Des Moines. The judge sentenced them to federal prison for three years of hard labor after they had been found guilty of the charges by separate juries.

✧ ✧ ✧

Emanuel and Melvin could have faced a five-year term plus a $10,000 fine. So we can see the courts were a little lenient. They ended up serving one year in prison and two years on parole.

Are we ready to stand up for our beliefs like they were? No matter what the outcome may be? This example again shows us how dedicated our parents were in their belief.

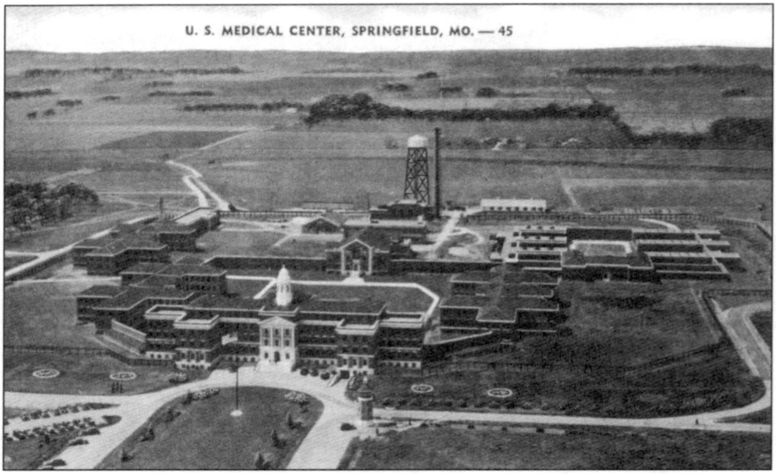

Chapter 14

# 1954 Felty Bontrager Farm

The time had come to make yet another move. It was hard to get ahead, having to move all the time. This time the Millers moved to the Felty Bontrager farm which consisted of only sixty acres. Livestock needed to be sold.

John informed his family that it was time to do something different for a change. After the move, he built a 16' x 24' building on runners so they could move it if need be. John started to fix combine canvas, shoes, harnesses, and many other items in the shop.

John also made a rig on a wagon gear where he mounted a Bearcat grinder and an Oliver power unit all in one. The rig was so heavy that three horses were needed to pull it on muddy days. John would fill silos with the rig as well as grind feed. In the winter, corn shocks were ground for silage for the milk cows.

The twins were fifteen years old now and able to handle any of the work on the farm. There wasn't enough work on this small farm to keep the boys busy at home.

Amos helped in the shop now that the fieldwork was caught up. One day John asked Amos, "Do you think you could run the shop if Mom and I took a little vacation to Indiana?"

"Oh, sure Dad," answered Amos, glad for the opportunity to run the shop by himself.

Plans were made and John and Susan left for a two-week vacation.

It was combining season, so it wasn't long before Amos had more work than he bargained for. Canvas slats needed to be repaired, so he stayed up late to get the orders done. Amos stayed so busy, the two weeks went fast.

After his parents returned, he told them, "Guess how much I made while you were gone? Five hundred dollars!"

"What?" Susan asked in astonishment.

"Yup—$500!"

"Wow, that's more than I ever made in two weeks," came the proud voice from John.

"Guess we'll have to leave more often," chuckled Susan.

During cultivating time, Amos would bring the horses in for water at the stock tank. He noticed there were too many minnows in the tank one evening. He confronted his brother Johnny about it.

"Johnny, don't put all those minnows in the water tank. "There's too many in there."

"Oh," said Johnny, "I don't put them all in there. I just put the big ones in there and swallow the little ones."

"You didn't swallow them, did you?" asked Amos, his eyes wide in wonder.

"I sure did! I can still feel them tickle in my tummy."

"Oh, yuck!" Amos gagged. Later Amos informed his dad about the minnow swallowing, and his dad took care of that!

That fall Susan's brother Noah Bontrager came to live with them for a while. His brothers and sisters took turns caring for him. He would get epileptic seizures once in a while. Once he had a seizure and fell, hitting his head on the coal bucket by the stove.

The twins enjoyed playing the number game with Noah. Numbers were written on pieces of cardboard about three-fourths of an inch square. The numbers were placed face down on the table and then mixed up. Each person would draw four numbers, placing them inside a book so the others couldn't see the numbers. You would then ask someone for a certain number you needed. If that person didn't have the number you asked for, you would then need to draw a number from the table. A person having four same numbers would turn them up on a pile. The first person to get rid of all their numbers won the game.

Another favorite rainy-day game was to make paper airplanes and sail them through the house at each other.

During the winter months, the boys would go to the field to get corn shocks, take them in and grind them up for silage for the cows. An axe was needed to cut the shocks loose from the frozen ground. Maggie, the farm dog, would tag along and chase after the mice when they would run out of the shocks.

Once they all had a surprise when a skunk came wandering out. Whew, Maggie! She smelled bad for about a week.

During the busy months of farming, Susan didn't get much help from the boys, so she hired a girl to help with the canning. That summer, she hired Amelia Mast to help her.

John and Susan had to make some decisions as there just wasn't enough income from the small farm to make ends meet. It was decided Andy would do the farming, and Amos would work out. It had been three years since Amos had worked out last. He now felt better prepared than he had three years earlier.

Amos was stronger than Andy due to the rheumatic fever Andy had at age five. Amos felt sorry for Andy and wished he could work out too.

Susan explained to Andy one day, "Now Andy, it's not that Amos is better than you, he is stronger, and that's why they ask for Amos."

"Sure, Mom, I know," came the reply.

The first place Amos worked out that time was at Levi Miller's. Levis were good friends of John and Susan. Levi was a minister in the Amish Church.

With his sixteenth birthday just around the corner, Amos felt a little uneasy working for Levi. He was afraid of doing something wrong.

Amos thought Levis had some nice looking girls and tried to show respect to them. He remembered his mother's advice one day. "Amos, you carry the milk buckets for those girls. Boys are much stronger, and so you need to show respect to women folk."

Amos felt closest to Alma, and they shared a lot. One day Alma said, "Amos, you're supposed to go home Wednesday night. Is it okay if I ride along?"

"Sure," Amos had answered. Now why did he need to go home, he wondered. When arriving home, he could see more company was there. They brought homemade ice cream and cake to celebrate the twins' birthdays.

Amos felt more grown up than ever by now as he drove back to Levi's with Alma. Alma was a year older than Amos and seemed like a big sister for him to look up to.

That summer Amos helped to build a new barn for Levi. He loved to go to the hay mow to yodel and sing his auctioneer song. It would echo, and he thought it sounded nice.

Amos collected quite a few songs from Alma that summer. They would sing a lot together and Amos enjoyed that. Later that fall, Alma got married to a young man named Monroe Mast

Amos had learned to enjoy working out. He found it easy to adjust to other people's ways. At least he thought so until his second job came along.

That next job took him twenty-five miles away, working for an English man. After working for him several weeks, Amos understood why the man had gone through six other hired hands. The guy was Catholic which Amos had no problem with, but it seemed to Amos he didn't live up to his beliefs. He would go to confession and early mass, then come back home and cuss Amos out for the rest of the day. Amos found out later that was why the other hired hands had quit. They wouldn't put up with that kind of language.

One morning this guy's dad was helping Amos get some cribs ready for corn. Amos hit his thumbnail with the hammer. A few cuss words slipped from Amos's tongue before he realized what he was saying.

The older fellow looked on in astonishment as he said, "Amos, I never expected to hear words like that coming from you."

Now Amos had been embarrassed. He answered, "I never talked like that before I started working for your son."

"I'll talk with him about it," the fellow promised.

This was a rough summer for Amos as he didn't get to go home every weekend. Amos got so nerved up that he didn't need to be called to get up in the mornings. As soon as a light was turned on, Amos was awake and would hurry to get dressed.

By the time Amos got to the barn, the guy was milking already. He was 6'4" tall and a very fast worker. It was hard for Amos to keep up with him. They milked twenty-seven cows.

They put the milk in ten-gallon cans. The cans were carried about 150 feet to the milk house to be placed in the cooler.

The man would carry two milk cans at a time. As tall as he was, he could hang his arms straight down to carry them and still keep them off the ground. Well, short little Amos had to raise his arms to keep the cans from dragging! Also he needed to stop and rest several times before he got to the milk house. Amos lost forty pounds that summer, and was getting to be a pretty good looking guy!

Amos wished the English man would treat his wife better. She was a very nice lady, and Amos felt sorry for her. If breakfast wasn't ready when they got to the house, the guy would slap his wife's behind, and she would say, "Ouch! That hurt!" Then he would slap her again and ask, "Did that hurt, honey?" This was not the kind of treatment Amos thought you should give someone you loved.

Usually by the time Amos had his plate filled, the other guy would be done eating already. Sometimes he would say, "You going to eat all day, Amos?" as he headed out the door. "Come on, let's go!" After he left, his wife would visit with Amos while he finished his breakfast in a hurry.

"Amos," she would say, "I hope you never treat your wife like that."

"No, ma'am. I could never treat my wife that way, and I'm sorry he treats you like that."

On some weekends, Amos was asked to watch their children when the couple went out for the evening. Or sometimes they would go away for a weekend, and Amos would end up doing all the chores yet. Then he would hear a lot of cussing again, accusing Amos of not milking right, and how the cows had not produced enough milk while they were gone. It seemed you just couldn't please this guy, no matter how hard you tried.

Combining time was here which proved to be another challenge. The man never stopped the combine long enough to unload, so Amos had to drive along beside him in the field with the wagon. Amos had to try to keep the same pace as the combine. If he decided to make a quick stop, and Amos kept going—out went the wheat on the ground. Another cussing session took place.

The father happened to come along one day when this took place again. He told his son, "Now if you'd use a little common sense and stop long enough to unload the hopper, that wouldn't happen!"

This was one time, Amos was pushed too far. Amos was fed up with all of this, so he blurted out, "If you can't stop long enough to unload the hopper with common sense, then you can find someone else to work for you! I've had all I can take!"

Both men looked surprised at Amos.

After that Amos worked for several Amish farmers. Then John got busier in the shop and needed Amos at home. It sure was a lot more enjoyable working at home alongside his dad.

But working out had been a good experience for Amos and helped him to grow up.

**Felty Bontrager Farm**

Chapter 15

# Cold Winter — Another Marriage

"Dad," said Emanuel as he entered the shop where his dad was busy repairing canvas.

"Oh, hi Emanuel," came John's cheerful greeting as he looked up from his work.

"I was just wondering if we could get Amos to do chores for us while we spend some time in Indiana?"

"Sure, I think we can spare him for a week," came the quick reply.

"Maybe you can send Amos over Saturday, and I'll show him around then."

Amos got the message that night and a few days later he headed over to Emanuel's. Chores consisted of milking six cows by hand, feeding calves, and taking care of some laying hens.

Amos stayed there the whole time Emanuels were gone. "Wow," Amos thought the first few days, "this is a little scary to be responsible for all of this by myself." The house was too quiet for Amos. He heard every little sound including the mice.

By Wednesday the temperature had begun to drop. Amos stacked extra wood inside and banked the fire a little heavier. The house had been an old schoolhouse. It had no partitions to divide the rooms. Long curtains hung from the ceiling to divide the rooms. Amos didn't think the house had any insulation as he could feel the wind come through the walls.

When Amos woke up the next morning he said to himself, "I think my nose is frozen!" Shivering all over as he got dressed, Amos looked up to see Mary's plants all drooping. Checking the stove out he found only a few red embers left. So he stoked the stove again and put on his coat to keep warm. "Br-r-r-r . . . it's cold," he shivered.

Checking the indoor thermometer, Amos said out loud, "Twenty-nine degrees! No wonder I'm cold!" He checked the outdoor thermometer and his mouth dropped. "Thirty-two degrees below zero! Whew!" he said out loud. It made him feel better to talk out loud even if there was nobody to hear or to answer him.

"Guess I'll make myself some breakfast before I chore," he thought. He walked over to the kitchen pump to wash his hands first. "Oh, no water." he said in disappointment. After breakfast, he headed for the barn all bundled up to face the cold.

The barn pump had frozen up too. Amos knew what he had to do now. He would need to make the six miles home to get his dad's blowtorch to thaw the pipes.

By the time he got home, his horse was completely white with frost, and Amos felt frozen! He put the horse in the barn and headed for the house to have a cup of coffee. After relating his troubles to his mother and getting warmed up again, he made his way back to Emanuel's.

It was 9:00 p.m. by the time he got the pipes thawed, chores done, supper over, stacked the stove with wood, and added more covers to the bed. By the next morning, nothing had changed. Again he needed to use the blowtorch to thaw the pipes. Again the thermometer read thirty-two degrees below zero. It stayed that way for the whole week. Boy, Amos had his work cut out for himself. Amos was looking forward to getting back home to Mom and Dad—and a warm house.

Was he ever glad to see Emanuel and Mary come home! "I'm sorry your plants froze, Mary," Amos apologized.

"Don't worry about that, they needed trimming anyhow."

"The next time you want to go someplace, please pick a warmer week," Amos kidded his brother Emanuel.

"That's what brothers are for!" Emanuel teased back.

✧ ✧ ✧

## Young Folks Activities

When Andy and I were growing up, some winter activities included ice skating down the river and playing hockey on a pond. Rook cards were a favorite when the weather turned too cold to skate.

When the youth went skating, sometimes they would skate eight miles down the river which usually took an hour, depending on the ice. They would skate real fast, then try to jump the logs frozen in the river. Occasionally someone would break through the ice getting their feet wet. If the ice was thin at places, they would walk the banks for a while.

When playing hockey, a tin can was used for the puck. The cans slid very fast. The hockey sticks were usually sought in the woods.

Once while playing hockey, someone knocked my feet out from under me causing a fall backwards, knocking me out. Coming to, I saw stars for a while. I ended up staying in the house the rest of the afternoon with a bad headache and a swollen head. On Monday, I had to make a trip to the doctor. X-rays showed a slight concussion. The doctor said I was fortunate it wasn't much worse.

In the summer, swimming and ball playing were enjoyed.

During the summer after a long day's work, the guys would go to the river to bathe and cool off. At the bend of the river, the water was the deepest. Jumping off the fifteen foot bank into the deep water was a real treat after a hard day's work.

After the Sunday evening Singing, some of the guys would sometimes go "cutting up" (visiting the dating couples). After checking out the pantry for baked goods, the guys would have fun with the dating couples, making it so they weren't alone.

Sometimes the pranks went a little too far, like unhitching the dating guy's horse and turning him out to pasture.

One night a few of the boys got carried away. They took off wheels on a buggy and rolled them into a ditch along the road. Then six guys hoisted the buggy about three-fourths of the way to the top of a windmill. They took ropes and tied the buggy to the windmill. When the dating guy left for home that night, he couldn't find his buggy. He borrowed a buggy from his girlfriend's folks to go home. Who would have thought to look up the windmill to find your buggy?

Another time, a group of boys pushed a threshing machine into the front yard, then went inside to pester the dating couple. The dating guy asked the boys to leave, so he could have some private time with his gal.

Most of the boys took the jokes good-naturedly, but a few did not.

✧ ✧ ✧

At the Millers, everyone was rushing around getting ready for a trip to Missouri for Ezra's wedding on September 1, 1955. The twins were quite excited as this was the first wedding they would have part in. Ezra had warned them ahead of time that things were different in Jamesport, Missouri than in Buchanan County, Iowa. The twins couldn't wait to see how different things actually were.

Train tickets were purchased, and the trip was made to Trenton. From there a taxi was taken to Barbara's house.

This was to be the first wedding taking place in the new settlement, so they thought that made it special. There were only twelve families living there at the time, that didn't include very many youth in the Church.

The buggies were very different than what Amos was used to in Iowa. They had sliding doors and upholstered interiors. In Iowa the young boys drove buggies with no tops. The married couples drove closed buggies, but had no fronts or doors.

The twins felt pretty grownup having partners at the wedding. They attended Church on Sunday and the Singing in the evening. Barbara had two sisters, Susie and Sadie who attended the Singing too. Andy got up enough nerve to ask Susie out for the evening. Amos was let down as he had his eye on Susie during the wedding.

Amos was thinking that Susie was one of the nicest gals he had ever seen. She was shorter than Amos, and a very good looking gal. Not that Amos had anything against Sadie, but something about Susie had made his heart skip a beat! Amos ended up asking Sadie out for his first date.

The young folks had played "walk-a-mile" after the Singing. That game was frowned upon in Iowa. The twins enjoyed the trip so much, the time to head back home came too soon.

After getting back home, Amos daydreamed a lot about the wedding and the trip to Missouri. Amos started to work out again, and Andy took care of the farming.

It was canning season once again, and Susan needed help. She hired a girl, Amelia Mast, to help her. Amos thought Amelia was a nice girl and after the dating experience in Missouri, he got up enough nerve to ask her out. She accepted and Amos was her first date. (The Amish called this "snitzing" when someone had their first date.)

Amos had thought, "This may be my future gal." But after a few dates, Amelia turned him down. Amos was let down but understood when Amelia said she would like to date other boys too.

"Guess this is all a part of growing up," Amos thought.

Chapter 16

# Bunker Hill Farm

Late in the fall after Ezra's wedding, they were informed they would need to look for another place by February 1956. Now it wasn't so easy finding another farm right away. Finally they found the Bunker Hill farm, but the house and outbuildings were so rundown that John had said, "The house isn't even fit to live in." John had made a deal with the owner for material and labor to be figured off the yearly rent.

December and January were very cold months to be working on the house. Sheetrock needed to be put up through the whole house. The job seemed never ending. Finally the second week of February, they moved in.

John had a contract made up, an agreement to let them live on the eighty acre farm for two years. This was their sixth move, and John and Susan were getting older. It grew more stressful each time.

When spring arrived, they worked on the outbuildings. Twenty inches were taken off one building because of being rotted out. A new footer was poured, and the building was lowered on top of two rows of cement blocks.

The building was then used as a chicken house. The chickens had been running loose until the building was ready. Eggs were found under the trees, in the barn, and other places. When it came time to round up the hens, they waited until dark. The hens produced well with a one hundred percent record in the new building.

About every two weeks, Amos would make a trip to the town of Hazleton to get feed for the chickens and buy groceries for his mother. There would still be $50 left, so the family income had increased. With the income from John's shop, they were finally able to make ends meet.

A new roof was put on the hip-roof barn. Amos was glad for Willie Yoder's help on the twenty-two foot high roof.

Andy did the plowing that year while Amos helped repair the buildings. After the repairs were completed, Amos went to work for Willie as a carpenter. He also helped bale hay for some of the English people.

Eleven-year-old Johnny and nine-year-old Joni helped more around the farm and in the house now too. There was a creek below the hill where Johnny spent a lot of time fishing. Amos couldn't remember any report of some big fish Johnny caught, but they might have been big in Johnny's eyes.

That spring Amos didn't have many dates but attended the Sunday evening Singings. He had asked a few girls out, but had been turned down. It seemed every time there was a visiting girl at the Singing, one of the other boys beat Amos and asked her out first.

Now Amos was getting lonely and thought no one cared for him by now! One Sunday evening, he asked Clara Bontrager out, and she accepted. Amos was surprised but glad she had. This helped Amos's courage in asking other girls out.

Sometime had passed without any dates. For a while, Amos joined the other boys in "cutting up" on Sunday evenings, but this got to be an old story, and Amos wasn't enthused with that.

One night they had nowhere to go, so one of the boys came up with an idea. "Amos, I think you should have a date with Lovina Hochstetler!"

"No thanks," came the answer from Amos.

"Aw, come on, Amos," they had pleaded. "She's a nice gal."

"I'm not interested, so just knock it off, okay?"

"But Amos—" they insisted.

"She won't accept anyhow, so I won't ask her," Amos replied. Not that he had anything against her, but she just wouldn't accept—he knew.

"Oh, you don't need to ask, we'll do the asking for you!"

Amos thought about this for a while. I guess if she said no, at least I wouldn't be embarrassed, he thought. Finally after some time, he said, "Okay, go ahead and ask, but I already know the answer."

The boys came back and told Amos that she had agreed to the date that evening.

They both had a good time, and Lovina had said, "Amos you're welcome to come back anytime you want."

The other boys had come to Lovina's home to cut up. Lovina's dad came out and asked the boys to leave. Some of them had been in the pantry looking for pies or baked goods, and when they heard the order to leave, they left through the pantry window.

The boys decided to get even with Lovina's dad. So they went to the chicken house, caught some chickens ,and turned them loose on the porch. Lovina's dad was so upset, he called the police. The police questioned Amos as to who did the damages. Amos informed them he knew the bunch, but didn't know exactly who did what.

None of the boys admitted to the damages done, so they all helped pay. Amos felt bad about the deal and had not asked Lovina out again.

A few months later, the boys asked Lizzie Hershberger if she'd accept a date with Amos. She agreed. There was Amos again furnishing a place for the boys to cut up. The boys helped themselves to pie, and Lizzie's dad didn't chase them off. They left in peace. Amos decided from now on he would do his own asking, so the boys wouldn't know about it. Amos was getting upset with how those boys were acting.

Amos wished they lived in Jamesport. He expressed his feelings to his mom and dad that he would like to move there because the young people seemed so caring there. Much more than in Iowa. His parents gave this much thought when they visited Jamesport again that fall.

Andy wasn't having any dates. He hadn't felt comfortable either. Andy spent a lot of time with his friend Junior Yoder, which left Amos alone quite often.

A challenge was soon to come to Amos making a change in his life—if only he knew.

It was a nice Sunday morning in late May of 1957. Everyone at the Millers had their chores done and were getting ready for Church. As the twins were getting the horses ready, Andy said, "Amos, let's just go in one buggy today."

“Okay,” said Amos, thinking this was unusual as they generally took separate buggies. Church was at Junior Yoder’s, Andy’s friend.

The morning church service had about the usual attendance. After Church, Junior and Andy decided to go on a drive. Andy went with his friend Junior, and Amos followed with his buggy. Amos wondered what those two were up to—they seemed kind of different today.

They ended up in a small town called Littleton. There was a small grocery store, a gas pump, and an outdoor theater. Andy and Junior went into the grocery store for some things, knowing they weren’t supposed to go to town on Sundays. Amos waited outside. He was thinking about what Andy had said that morning about just taking one rig.

When Andy and Junior returned from the store, Andy said, “Amos there’s a movie on at the theater tonight.”

“Yeah, why don’t we stay and watch it?” Junior suggested.

Amos hadn’t said anything and didn’t like the movie idea, but he stayed with the boys. After a while, Amos mentioned to Andy, “We’d better go to the Singing tonight, and we’d better go now or we’ll be late. You know Mom and Dad wouldn’t approve of us going to the movies.”

“You go ahead, and Junior and I will come later,” Andy replied.

When Amos got to the Singing, everyone wanted to know where Junior and Andy were. Amos told them, “They’ll be here later.”

Amos couldn’t keep his mind on singing. What were Junior and Andy up to? After the Singing, the boys filed out and were having their fun watching who took which girl home so they’d know where to go to cut up that night. Amos was pretty quiet that night and didn’t feel like cutting up. Andy and Junior still had not showed up at the Singing.

Amos decided to go home early as he couldn’t get Andy off his mind. They were so used to doing things together.

Coming home, Amos unhitched the horse and put him in the barn. Making his way to the house, he figured surely Andy was home by now, and he’d talk to him about what he had done. Going upstairs, he found no trace of Andy. By now Amos wondered, "What is that boy up to? Surely he'll be home later on." Amos couldn't get to sleep right away. He kept thinking of all the events that had taken place today.

The next morning, John called the boys, "Amos, Andy, come on, chore time."

Amos got up, but discovered Andy was gone. What would he tell Mom and Dad now? While getting dressed, Amos dreaded what lay ahead when his parents found out Andy wasn't there. As Amos turned to go downstairs, he glanced down at Andy's shoes. A piece of paper was sticking out. Now what was that all about? His heart skipped a beat as he took the paper in his trembling hands.

Tears were streaming down his cheeks as he read, "This is Andy. I have left home and don't come looking for me. I won't come back home if you come after me."

Amos flung himself on the bed, and through blinding tears sobbed, "Oh, Andy, why? Lord, why? Why . . . why . . . why?" But no answer came.

The twins would soon be eighteen years old. How Amos was torn at his brother's leaving. They had always been together, done everything together. What had happened? Why didn't Andy tell him what he was going to do?

Gathering himself together, he knew he needed to get downstairs to tell his parents.

When Amos got downstairs, he handed the note to his mother with tears in his eyes. He knew this would break their hearts.

Tears flowed unchecked down Susan's cheeks as she read the note out loud. Amos would never forget the sad expressions on everyone's faces that morning.

That morning John extended the morning prayer to half an hour. After prayer they headed for the barn in silence to get the chores done.

After breakfast John asked Amos, "Would you get a horse hitched up for me? I want to go see if Junior's home. Maybe he knows where Andy is." Coming back, John informed the family that Junior was gone too.

The first few weeks were hard on everyone, not knowing where Andy had gone. Amos knew he had to keep going to keep his mind occupied. He tried not to mention Andy's name too often.

There was a lot of spring plowing to be done. Amos tried to keep his mind on the plowing as much as possible which was hard to do. Questions, questions. "Why . . . why . . . why?" Two weeks had passed with no word from Andy.

Amos couldn't read the German Bible or prayer book but that didn't keep him from praying in his own words. During the times of plowing, Amos would rest his horses about six times. Each time, Amos would kneel and pray that God would give him peace of mind and reveal Andy's whereabouts, letting him know Andy was okay.

After receiving that peace of mind, Amos kept praying that God would change Andy's heart to come home again.

One day after Amos had pleaded to God to reveal his brother's whereabouts, his answer came. His mom and dad had been informed that same day that someone had seen Andy in a town about fifteen miles from there.

Amos now thanked God over and over again for answering his prayers. Amos felt closer to God than ever before.

The next morning John and Susan sought the authorities to see if they would take them to where Andy was staying. Arriving at the farm where Andy was working, they were informed Andy wasn't there. After some time in conversation, the people admitted he was there, but Andy didn't want to talk to his parents.

John then turned to the authorities for help in bringing their son home. They were told Andy was eighteen years old, and therefore considered an adult. No, they couldn't force him to go home. John and Susan returned home with saddened hearts. Amos would never forget the sad look in his mother's eyes as she told Amos about the incident.

Susan's concern now was, "Had Andy registered when he turned eighteen? Would he get drafted like Emanuel, and then they'd have another ordeal to go through?"

Amos's faith had grown stronger because God had answered his prayers. So his prayers continued, asking God to bring Andy home.

As Amos continued the spring plowing in the weeks that followed, he was expecting his prayers to be answered. One Friday night, Amos had a dream that Andy was coming home on Saturday. He knew this was God answering his prayers. The next morning, he told his parents, "Andy's coming home today."

"How do you know that?" asked his mother in astonishment. Amos then shared how God revealed this to him in a dream the night before.

"Mom, fix Andy's favorite food today," Amos had suggested.

Amos's spirits had lifted. He kept watching the road for a sign of Andy. Soon a pickup came in sight. Amos's heart beat faster. Could that be Andy coming home?

"It's Andy! Andy's home!" Amos announced as the pickup turned into the drive. What a joyful reunion they had!

Amos again thanked God for answering his prayers. His faith grew stronger yet. This was one of the happiest weekends they had together in a long time as they shared their love for each other.

If only Amos could tell everyone how happy he felt. A part of him had been missing. There had been a closeness there that he hadn't felt with his other brothers. This experience made Amos love his twin brother more than ever.

Andy had told his family he still planned on working for the farmer and would come home on weekends.

Amos prayed that this wouldn't happen to other young people. He didn't want other parents to go through what his parents went through. "May God bless those who search to love and serve Him," he prayed.

✧ ✧ ✧

I would like to share this prayer with all teenagers. I am sure if you lead a life like this prayer you will receive a blessing and also make your parents very happy.

## A Prayer from a Teenager

**Oh God, help make me be a better kid. Help me to love my parents like I should. Help me understand that just because they don't give me everything I ask for, it doesn't mean they don't love me. In my heart I know it means they love me enough to say no.**

**May I always believe that my parents do the best they can. Help me not to compare what they do for me with what they do for my brothers and sisters. Sometimes I need to be reminded that we are all individuals with different needs.**

**Give me the good sense to accept criticism from my parents without losing my cool. They have been around a lot longer than I have and know what is best for me.**

**Help me, Lord, not to blow up when my parents ask me where I'm going or when I will be home. They aren't being nosy. They really care.**

**Help me to be patient and answer their questions without putting them down. They grew up in a different era and many things about our culture are strange to them.**

**Especially, Dear Lord, help me to respect them. They aren't perfect, but neither am I. Help me to be courteous to them. It's funny how we treat the people closest to us with a lot less respect than we give strangers.**

**Finally, God, bless my parents for all the things they do for me, and help me love them as much as they love me.**

***–Author unknown***

Wouldn't it be a wonderful teenage world today, if all teenagers would live a life according to this prayer?

Bunker Hill Farm

Chapter 17

# Challenge for Amos

This had been a very challenging year for Amos, with the experience of Andy's departure and the way the young folks were. He tried to do what was right but it seemed things just didn't turn out like he wanted.

Now another challenge was at hand concerning the family dog, Maggie. She was getting old and weak. She just lay around and wouldn't eat. After being of good service to the family for ten years, Amos knew her end was near. He needed to accept the fact that Maggie was dying. He would never forget the time she had saved his life.

The day came soon that Maggie's life was over. Amos took her to the back pasture and buried her where she had done most of her work. This had been a sad day for Amos. He felt as if a part of him had been buried too. But life must go on, even if it was like losing one of the family.

Amos didn't have much idle time that summer with the farming in his hands. He also helped others bale hay. John was very busy in his shop and didn't have time to help Amos. Even the milking was mostly up to Amos. John helped when he could.

God had other plans for Amos. If only Amos knew. He tried to keep content with what God's plans were for him at this time. God had lifted his spirits in the past few months.

Amos would soon be blessed with some happy days ahead.

It was now the first week in July. Amos received news of three visiting girls in the area. He wasted no time in finding out where they were staying and who they were. Amos wanted to have a good opportunity to ask one of them out before any of the other boys got the chance.

Amos learned their names were Inez and Verna Yoder and Susie Miller. Susie was his sister-in-law Barbara's sister, and he remembered her from the wedding. He took the first opportunity and asked her for a date. She accepted and said she had planned to visit his parents while on this trip.

The girls stayed in the area for two weeks which gave Amos a chance to date Susie several times. Susie was a good listener and very understanding as Amos shared some of the things that had taken place the past month.

The two weeks came to an end, too soon for Amos. He got up enough courage to ask Susie, "Would you answer my letters if I wrote to you while you're in Indiana?" Susie would be working for her brother Chris while she was there.

She replied, "Sure, I will." So this is how they started out as friends. Amos felt Susie was someone he wanted to get to know better.

Susie had felt sorry for what Amos had been through. That was why she had agreed to answering his letters.

After spending that little time with Susie, Amos's future looked brighter. Work went better knowing he would have someone to confide in, and Susie would support him. It didn't take long to know that she was a real caring person.

Amos's spirit lifted when one day soon after her departure. He received a postcard Susie had written while waiting for her bus in Chicago on her way to Indiana. The card was stamped July 25, 1957.

*Dear Friend,*

*Greetings of love. I will in a hurry scribble a few lines. We have to wait two hours here at the Chicago depot for our Indiana bus. But time is about due, am glad when we get out of here.*

*Thought I would drop you a few lines now. Will write more when I get there. Card is full and time is at end.*

*So long, just me, S.M.*

The card meant a lot to Amos. It showed him she was true to her word, and she cared . He could hardly wait for his first letter. He was on "cloud nine."

Amos didn't need to wait long, for the letter arrived soon after. This seemed too good to be true. He stopped work to read the letter.

*LaGrange, Ind.*
*July 25, 1957*

*Dear Amos,*

*Greetings of purest love through Jesus Christ. Will try to write a few lines to you tonight yet. I was late in getting out of town soon enough to write and put it in the mail today. There wasn't anybody in LaGrange to meet us when we got off the bus. We had to wait an hour before anyone picked us up. By the time we got to brother Harveys, the mailman had already gone. Don't know when I will go to brother Chris's yet. I still haven't received a letter from home, seems they always wait two weeks before they write me a letter.*

*Hope you and the rest are all sailing in the boat of good health. I'm just like usual except for a little sleepy. Did catch up with some of my loss of sleep today.*

*Back again, if I keep at it, I guess I'll finally get this letter done before the mailman goes.*

*We sure had a time again yesterday on our way to Independence. Just a little before we came to Independence the one back buggy wheel started going kind of jumpy. At first we just had a little fun about it, but finally we decided to see why it was doing that, just what do you think we saw? Over half the spokes were out of the wheel, so these spokes would come on the ground and make the bumpy ride.*

*So we got off and pretty soon a car came along, they said they would take us along to Independence. We unhitched the horses and tied them to the fence along the ditch. This lady in the car said she would take Elizabeth and the children to some Amish to find the wheel, or she would also take them home whichever she wanted to do. Sure wonder how she got home.*

*That buggy wheel had been that way a long time but he hadn't told her until yesterday. I know she wouldn't have started out with it if she had known it was that bad, sure was worried about her.*

*Well I reckon you wouldn't mind reading something else, but do I know anything else to write? ha I wouldn't mind going to brother Chris's tonight, but don't know if I will or not as it's pretty early yet.*

*Well if plans hold out and I can find someone to go with me I will be seeing you again in September. Don't know how long I'll stay, maybe two or three weeks. Depends on how things go at one other place. Well supper is ready and nerws is scarce, so I will step on the brakes until next round. ha*

*Love, Luck, and Best Wishes,*
*Susie Ann Miller*

*P.S. Excuse all mistakes and take them for hugs. Answer soon, will watch the mailbox everyday. Those girls sure had a good time packing my suit case. When I got to Indiana, I found four corn cobs and a package of salt in my suitcase. ha Have to get this in the mail. Harvey's have thrashers for dinner so you know what I will be doing today.*

Susie's letter showed Amos so much more—how Susie really was. Her concern for others, her caring, her good humor, and her true love for Jesus Christ. How could a person like him not want to answer a wonderful letter like the one he received from Susie?

Amos's letter in response:

*July 27, 1957*

*Dear Susie,*

*Greetings of best love. How does this find you in health? I'm okay am feeling fine but would be a little happier if you were here. We have been thrashing these last days, but today it rained in the afternoon. I came home and went to Oelwein, didn't have much business but went anyway so I'd have something to do. ha*

*What have you been doing these days? Catching up with your sleep! ha Have you found a good job yet? Hope you have, wish you luck in finding a good one. What are you going to do tomorrow? Guess I am going to Church at Willie Yoder's, then in evening, go to Singing.*

*There's really nothing else to do if you aren't here. Sure wish you could be here now. You don't know how much I have missed you since you left for Indiana, guess I'll make it till September. ha*

*I don't know if my mom told you or not, but they are planning to go down to Jamesport, Missouri around the first of November. They said I could go down later on. Last night I got the chance to make a quick dollar. Christi and I took a load of oats over to a different farm for Enos Mullet. It was after dark when we left so we didn't get back home till 11:45 PM. I'm kind of sleepy tonight. Will try to finish this letter when I come home from the Singing.*

*Here I am again, got back from Church about an hour ago. There was a visiting preacher there, but I don't know what his name was. What are you going to do tonight? Guess I will wait here till the folks come home, then eat supper and go to the Singing. I went home from Church without eating dinner. The boys teased me, they said I probably had to go home and write a letter. My news box is MT, hope to do better next time. Look forward to hearing from you soon. Was at the Singing tonight, would've enjoyed myself a lot better if you would've been there. You can take my mistakes as hugs.*

*With best wishes and ever lasting love,*

*a friend, Amos Miller*

Amos was patiently waiting for a response to his first letter to Susie. Was he too forward in letting her know of his love for her? Would Susie decide not to answer any more letters?

What did the future hold? Only God knew.

## Part II — Young Adult Years

Chapter 18

# Romance Letters

Amos was still waiting patiently for a letter from Susie. He was still wondering if he had been too forward in his first letter to her—should he have let her know how he felt?

One evening while he was washing up for supper, his mother announced, "Amos, you had a letter in the mail today!" Amos stopped washing and looked up to meet his mother's gaze in the mirror. His heart did a little "flip flop" and then he dared ask, "Who was it from?"

"It didn't have a return address," she smirked, "but it looks like a girl's writing."

Amos could hardly contain himself until supper was over. He picked up the white envelope and headed upstairs. He hugged the letter to his chest and prayed, "Dear God, is this my answer?"

He carefully opened the precious letter and read . . .

*Aug. 1, 1957*

*Dear Amos,*

*Greetings of purest love through Jesus Christ.*

Susie had underlined love. "Aw . . . purest love," Amos thought, "yes . . . " That told him she had the love of God in her heart. (When we have the love of God within us, it is easy to show others how much we care for them.) Amos read on . . .

*"Hope this finds you fine as I wouldn't want it any different. I'm as usual except lonesome for you! I'm working for my brother Chris now and feel right at home. I'm not sure how much they'll pay me but whatever they can afford is fine. I was at Church last Sunday but have no plans for this Sunday. September is a little*

*ways off yet, but it will be here before we know it. I wish I could see you tomorrow so I wouldn't need to write this letter.*

"Oh, I wish so too . . . ," thought Amos.

*Your mother hadn't mentioned anything about their going to Missouri in November but maybe I can travel with them then. I'll need to go to Buchanan to see you and take in a few weddings! (I hope you don't mind!)*

"Don't mind?" thought Amos. "Girl, if only you knew! Well, I'll write and let you know. I don't mind one bit!" He read on . . .

*The weddings will be William Yoder and Susan Bontrager. Also Sam Miller and Lydia Bontrager. But please Amos, don't tell anyone as they aren't published yet.*

*Sunday will be so lonesome here without you.*

*I had a letter from home today. I left two weeks ago and this was my first letter. Don't you think that's been quite long - - not hearing from them?*

Amos thought about that . . . "I think she loves her family and misses them. What a caring, loving girl she must be."

*I only found nine mistakes in your letter and that wasn't very many kisses -- make more mistakes in your next letter!*

*With love,*
*Susie Ann Miller*

Amos re-read the letter three times that night. He would sleep with it buried under his pillow. He wanted it as close to his heart as possible.

Amos decided to write to Susie.

Aug. 3, 1957

Hi there Honey,

Greetings of purest love, want to answer your welcome letter which I read again today. I can hardly wait till the time comes that I can see you again. Well, you gave me a little surprise in your letter about coming out. I knew Williams were getting married as I got a letter from them the other day. In his letter he asked me if you and I would be table waiters. Of course, I figured it's all right with me if it is with you. How about it Honey? So I guess if you come for their wedding, you will have to come before September 1st, which suits me fine, which I hope it does you too.

They probably will get published *[announced in church]* on Aug. 18-19, 1957. Their wedding day is Aug. 29. Mother said that his grandpa Urias Yoders might be invited. We will let you know so that maybe you could come out with them. I was hoping you could be here Monday, the week of the 29th, so we could have a few days together before the wedding, whatever suits you the best. Whenever you come, let me know so I can meet you at the bus depot.

Yes, we finished thrashing Friday night and I am glad we are done too. This morning Dad and I went to Hazleton to get feed and groceries. I also got some special tacks for the upholstery on my buggy, want to have it all fixed and painted before you come. I am invited over to Levi Millers - - they told me to bring my Rook cards along. So guess you know what we will be doing. Wish you were here to help us. I got home from the Singing about fifteen minutes ago, I took Joni's girls' home first.

Love, Luck, and Best Wishes
From a Loving friend, Amos Miller

Susie was busy hanging up clothes on the line when she saw the mailman stop. "Oh!" she thought, "Wouldn't that be wonderful if I'd have a letter already? . . . But, Lord, I know I need to be patient . . . He probably just got mine last week, and he won't write so soon again. Did I write my feelings for him too boldly?"

Running to the mailbox before going in for another basket of clothes, she opened the lid and peeked inside. "Wow! I don't believe this," Susie said to herself.

She tucked the white envelope inside her dress pocket and would read it later in her room. It didn't take Susie long to finish the laundry now. Her feet seemed to have springs in them.

Later she read every word carefully . . .

That night Susie took out her paper and a pen and wrote an answer to the letter she had just received from Amos.

Aug. 7,1957

Dear One,

Greetings of love. It sure was a welcome letter I received from you. I was just waiting for Wednesday to peep around the corner, but it was a little slow getting here. I received three letters Wednesday, from you, my folks, and Katie Schmucker. Of course your letter was the first one I read. I don't have very much time to write as we are going to Chris's neighbors for ice cream, will finish this when I get back.

I also received a letter from William Susan, she wants to know if we are hung up with each other. ha She said she means business. Yep, that is all right with me to be table waiter. Wonder what you will do Sunday. I would like to go to Ashley over Sunday, don't know how I'll go yet. I might go on the bus. Guess I will go to Uncle Joe's today with Chris's buggy as Amanda is too busy to go along.

I have planned to leave on the 26th or 27th. I will probably leave the 26th as they have changed the bus schedule and the bus fare's have raised too. It is a little over two weeks yet and I'll be seeing you. Well, news is all - - answer soon.

A loving friend,
Susie Ann Miller

Amos was excited when he received yet another letter from Susie. He couldn't wait to have part in the wedding with her. Their love was growing with each letter. A few days later he wrote . . .

August 11,1957

Dearest Loved One,

Want to answer your welcome letter which I received Saturday. Wonder how this finds you in health? I am okay and feeling fine today. I had a little mishap yesterday, at noon when I let the colt out. It was caught with its rope. When I got the rope loose, it wanted to go out right away before I had its halter off. The colt backed around till it stepped on my foot and got my foot out of place.

I didn't think too much about it when it happened. This afternoon, I was sitting on my feet painting my buggy, when I got done I could hardly walk on my foot. Dad gave me a foot treatment. Then I soaked my foot in hot water and put some muscle aid on it and went to bed. This morning it was kind of sore to start with but it's feeling better. Anyway, I feel spry and happy, but would enjoy myself better if you were here. Anyway, don't worry about me. You probably want to hear something else by now. We got a letter from Susan the other day, she said she was glad that we would be table waiters. She also wrote that she hopes she didn't hurt my feelings for telling me to let my hair grow longer for the wedding. I told Mom I could even make a pony tail if I have to. ha ha

Mother said she wouldn't be surprised if you would have to wear an Iowa covering the day of the wedding. Susan wrote they want everything to be in ordnung *[ in order]*. I told Mother you would look kind of funny in an Iowa covering, don't you think so? Let me know when you are going to leave and what town to meet you. Also let me know what time you will get here. I wouldn't care if you came after dark, that way not everybody would see us.

Did you get someone to come with you? I hope you won't have to travel alone. I would feel better if someone came with you. Monday, I need to put the last coat of paint on my buggy. Then Tuesday I want to wax it and also line the box with material I had left from the seat. Guess I will have it all slicked up by the time you get here.

Today there was a visiting preacher from Kalona, Iowa in our Church, his name was Mose Yoder. It's after 3 PM. I didn't stay to eat dinner so I could come home and write your letter. Brother Emanuels are coming over for supper tonight. Singing is at Willie Yoder's tonight, if you were here we could just walk to the Singing. Bet you couldn't guess what I dreamed about last night? You said you decided to come to Iowa quicker, but when I woke up you weren't here, so guess it was one of those sweet dreams. Hope to hear from you soon.

From your Loving Sweetheart,
Amos Miller

On the outside of the envelope Amos wrote: *Over the hills and far away, I think of you every day.* Amos was on cloud nine by now. His Dad accused him of being in "Dreamland."

Another letter from Susie found its way to Amos's mailbox.

Aug. 16, 1957

Dear Sweetheart,

Greetings of love. Want to answer your ever so welcome letter which I received today. Boy I was really disappointed Wednesday and yesterday when the mailman went, and I didn't get a letter from you. I thought I could hardly live through the rest of the day.

I know now why it didn't come until today. You put R#1 on instead of R#2 so it was mis-sent. You will probably feel the same way until Monday, the day you will get this letter. Guess I could've written anyway even if I didn't have your letter yet, but anyway I didn't. Am sorry I kept you waiting so long for your letter, but hope you understand.

Hi darling, am ready to finish your letter now, but is later than I figured it to be. Am a little happier tonight than I was the last two days. ha You know what? I am really anxious for this next week to hurry past. I don't know for sure yet which day I will come but it will be in the morning at 9 a.m. when I get to Independence. Guess you will have to get me there because if I want to go to Hazleton, I'll have to wait until 8:40 in the evening to leave Independence. I want to go to Ashley tomorrow evening and stay until Monday. When I get back from there, I can let you know when I will be coming. There is a chance that Inez Yoder will come with me. You can tell Emanuel Mary that her mother isn't coming as I got a card from her yesterday.

Yep, I didn't get to Ashley last Sunday. Dave's girls came here. Say Honey, next time you see Ervin Chupp tell him to write to Verna Yoder. I know she will answer him. You can tell him I told you if you want to. I just re-read your letter. Do your folks know about these letters that are going from one to the other? ha I was just wondering and don't care if they do.

Was looking for a letter from William Susan, but haven't received one yet, was kind of anxious to hear from her. I told Chris Amanda if I have to wear an Iowa covering, I'd tell Susan that they wouldn't have to get any for me. I would get your mother to help me make one that would fit me. Think it would suit your mother? Ask your mother and let me know. I suppose I will probably also have to wear an Iowa holsduch and schatz *[cape and apron]*. Hoped I could wear my own clothes. But if I can't, I just can't. ha We had company tonight, my Uncle Joe's, so that's why it's so late for me to write your letter tonight. With my best love to you.

Your Sweetheart
Susie Ann Miller

Susie hadn't known what to expect when Amos's letter had come three days later than usual. All kinds of thoughts passed through her mind. Was this Amos going to treat her like her first Amos did? She wrote to another Amos for a while and one day—there just weren't any more letters coming to her. She never knew why. How Susie rejoiced when another letter came from Amos Miller.

Amos answered Susie's last letter right away.

Aug. 19, 1957

Dear Sweetheart,

Greetings of my best love to you. Received your very welcome letter today. I could hardly wait until Monday to get a letter from you. I sure wondered Sat. why I didn't get a letter from you. I was a lot happier today when I received your letter. Wonder what you are doing to make the time go fast. I am making hay and all kinds of other work but seems time doesn't go too fast at that, as I am thinking of you. At dinner today as we were eating, I asked why they don't send cabbage over to me. Then they said that I had some already, but I didn't find out when I got it. Guess I was thinking too much of your letter and about you coming out here, so that I forgot myself.

Yesterday I went to southeast Church to hear if William and Susan got published to be married. When I got there, there was nobody there, because they had Church on Sat. instead. Boy, was I disgusted when I found out, if I had known I wouldn't have gone down there. So then I went to Danny Kauffman's. Danny told me they and Fred Gingrich's boys were invited over to Ervin Chupp, so I went over to Ervin's too.

Well, sweetheart, about getting a wedding present for Williams, you don't have to get one if you don't want to. My mother got a dinner set for $2 and said if you want to pay half you and I could give it to them from the both of us. It is four place settings and is a nice blue in color. Here I am again, I had supper so want to finish your letter. Mother said it would be okay with her to help you make an Iowa covering. Mother said she had enough material to make one but that the material might be thicker than what you want. She said if it's too thick for you maybe you can get some that you want. You asked if we heard from Andy. No we haven't since the first time. Mom and Dad both wrote him a letter a week ago today. Okay, Honey, I will tell Ervin Chupp that he should write Verna Yoder a letter, he will probably be tickled at the chance. ha ha Yes, my folks know about our letters, but they haven't read any of them. But they don't care, they acted like they were glad I had somebody to write to like you, sweetheart. I am glad too, much more than they are. Hope to be hearing from you before Sunday, so I know where to meet you. Honey, don't worry, I'll be there probably a few minutes early watching for you, sweetheart. Looking forward to seeing you soon.

Good night, with my Best Love to you,
Your Sweetheart, Amos Miller

Susie wrote a letter before she received Amos's letter. She wanted to be sure he received it in time so he knew when to pick her up.

Aug. 21, 1957

Dearest One,

Greeting of purest Love. Will scribble a few lines for you tonight. I haven't received your letter yet, but really didn't expect any until tomorrow. Thought I would write tonight and send it tomorrow to be sure you would get it in time to come after me. My friend Inez Yoder will be coming with me. I will leave here Monday the 26th in the evening at 8:20. Will arrive in Independence Tuesday the 27th in the morning at 9:00. So hope to be seeing you there. Why don't you take the top buggy to come after us. That way not everybody would see us.

They would see us go, but they might not know who it is. ha I got a letter from William Susan today. They said that they have a dress, holsduch and schatz there for me. She didn't mention about a covering, so maybe I can have my own, but doubt it. You know, Honey, I am kind of anxious to be in Iowa close to you. Chris Amanda said that I had zeitlang *[lovesickness]* last Wednesday, Thursday, and Friday till I got my letter from you on Friday. She said after I had my letter I seemed like myself again. I knew I was a little upset but I didn't think she would notice it. But that is the way it goes. One of these days I will have to start getting my suit case packed again. I don't think I was ever more anxious to get my suitcase packed than I am this time.

Boy just think of it, only a few more days and we will be seeing each other again. Seems I can't think of very much more to write. If I had your letter I probably could think of more. I got the nicest little gift today. Bro. Chris and family gave me a little travel alarm clock, one that stands up in the case. I was wanting one like that a long time already, now finally I have one. You will have to see all my other presents when I get there. Yesterday I packed a box full that I couldn't get into my suitcase, so I'm sending it home. I guess tomorrow will be the last time that I will hear from you for a few weeks. So I hope to have a big fat letter tomorrow. Boy I can't help but think of you every day. Good night Darling. Be seeing you soon.

A Loving Sweetheart,
Susie Ann Miller

After receiving a letter like this, Amos was really thrilled to know that Susie felt the same way he did about her. Those next few days sure went by slow. It was a blessing that God had answered his prayers for someone like Susie. It all seemed too good to be true. He thanked the Lord every day for his blessings and prayed for the future relationship they would have. Amos knew now that he had found his true companion and could hardly wait for them to be together.

Chapter 19

# Special Reuniting

The day finally arrived to meet Susie at the bus depot. Susie had written Amos to bring the top buggy to pick her up. Amos had already written her he would be bringing the top buggy (so no one could see them), so that told Amos they thought alike.

Amos left early to meet Susie. Arriving, he checked his watch, muttering to himself, "It's 8:50—just ten more minutes, and I'll see her!" Oh, he couldn't wait. His heart throbbed as he saw the bus arrive. An elderly couple stepped off first, then a few other people—and the door closed.

"What? But Susie—you need to step off too." A few minutes later, the bus pulled away, and Amos's heart sank. Now what? He made his way inside the building to talk to the ticket agent.

"Sir, what time does the next bus come in?" Amos asked.

Looking at the time schedule, the agent answered, "Three o'clock."

"Thank you, Sir," Amos answered, turning away and heading for his buggy. He sat on the buggy awhile deciding what to do. Should he go home or wait here? After some thought, he decided to head back home.

What a long day until it was time to head back. At 2:00 p.m., Amos headed toward Independence once more. The bus was on time. This time Susie stepped down and looked around for Amos. Their eyes met and spoke of their love for each other.

Amos wanted to run to her with open arms and hug and kiss her, but both were taught—you don't do that in public. Amos took Susie's suitcase as he said, "Hello." Inez followed them to the parked buggy.

Before they started out, Amos grabbed Susie and kissed her. Susie did not object even though Inez looked on.

"You two look like some young love birds," Inez had said.

"We are," Amos answered with a grin.

It was almost dark when they got home and Susie and Inez both spent the night there. The next day they took Inez to see some of her friends. At last they were alone to spend time together.

They both had a good time at the wedding. The next day, Amos took Susie over to Emanuel's to help out.

While at Emanuel's Susie wrote Amos.

Dear Sweetheart,

Greetings of love to you. Emanuel said it would be plenty late in the evening to bring me over to your place. So I guess it is up to you, Sweetheart, to come after me Thursday evening. It would suit best to have a date Thursday than almost any other night. Of course, we could date any other night also from there on. We would surely want to have more than two more dates, wouldn't we?

OK, Darling, be seeing you Thursday evening and don't let them talk you out of it. It is mailman time.

With Sincere Love, A Sweetheart,
Susie Ann Miller

Amos wouldn't let anyone talk him out of picking up Susie on Thursday evening. After being table waiters and spending time together, they felt a stronger love for each other. They had talked about what the future held for them. It would be quite awhile before they could be together for the rest of their lives. Only three more weeks to spend time with each other for now.

Amos's parents had planned a trip to Missouri on October 7th. It was decided that Susie would travel with them. The parting was so hard, but they both promised to write to each other, and that would make it easier. Susie wrote a card when they got to Des Moines, Iowa. She wrote they got on the train in Oelwein at 7:00 but didn't leave the station until 7:40 p.m.

Amos thought the next few days were so long until he received a letter from Susie. Amos was keeping busy with the shop, the chores, and taking care of his little brothers, Johnny and Joni. He knew there were some slow months ahead until they would get to see each other again.

The day finally came when Amos received Susie's first letter after she got home.

Oct. 8, 1957

Dear One,

Greetings of purest Love. Want to let you know I came home safe and sound. We got a taxi in Trenton and dropped your folks off at Ezra's after they dropped me off at home. I feel pretty good this morning except a little sleepy. ha How are you this morning, Honey? Suppose kind of lonesome. Boy, I know about how you feel because I sure miss you this morning.

My mother and sister Sadie are in Johnson, they will be home this PM sometime. You can just know how I felt and still feel - - coming home and then Mom not here.

Hope the time won't be too long for you while your folks are gone and till you come down here.

With Love From a True Loving friend,
Susie Ann Miller

Receiving a letter like this gave Amos the strength to continue on, knowing he would have future inspiring letters to encourage him. He responded to Susie's letter.

Oct. 10, 1957

Dearest Loved One,

Hope this finds you in the best of health. I am as usual. I have been busy in the shop since my folks are gone. I have also been working on the henhouse to get it done.

Well we got invited to a wedding since you went home. It's my cousin Sam Miller and Ruby Miller in Centreville, Mich. Well, you said Honey you hope that the time goes fast for me. Vel*[well]*, it went kind of faster the last days than I was afraid it would. But it sure is lonely when I'm by myself all day.

You know, last night when we went to bed, it was kind of cold, so I went to the east room to get a blanket. Then I saw the blanket was still on the bed that I had put on there for you. Sure thought I'd have to see you there, but you weren't there. ha I wished you would have been here to put the blanket on me. I am sure it would have warmed me up better.

Good morning, the school bus just went by so you know about what time it is. I don't have any work in the shop today, so guess I will work on the henhouse again. Must close and get to work. With my Best wishes and Love to you.

Your true Loving Sweetheart,
Amos J. Miller

Amos knew the days ahead would be long until he would receive another letter from Susie. He was looking forward to when his folks would come home so he could find out if they bought a place in Jamesport. He was looking forward to the day the family would move to Missouri, so Susie and he could see each other on a weekly basis instead of writing letters.

Amos knew that letters helped a lot—it's what keeps a person going till you meet each other again. The most encouraging words in Susie's letters were "purest love" she said she had for him. Those words were very uplifting to him, knowing she gave her whole heart to him to love.

Amos received Susie's next letter on October 16th.

Oct. 14, 1957

Dear Sweetheart,

Greeting of purest Love. Your letter came Saturday but I didn't get it till Sunday morning. I was at Ezra's Friday and Saturday. When I got home Saturday evening they hadn't got the mail. So Sunday morning on the way to Church we picked up the mail and sure enough there was your letter. I thought the week would never come to an end, but after I had read your letter, I felt better.

Wonder how you are in health? Me? I'm just as usual. Hope you are too, would be sorry to hear different.

I was in gros gma *[communion service]* yesterday and it was 5 p.m. already when Church was out. Boy I thought I could hardly sit anymore. But sure wished you were here or I there last night. My arms were oh, soooo empty last night and the night was so long and blue without you.

It is only 2 1/2 more months until January. I suppose the time will go pretty fast with all the work that is ahead. Anyway, I hope to see you some time in the near future.

What are you doing, honey? Do you have the hen house finished now? How much corn do you have to husk?

There is just one thing I don't like when you will be living here and that is that you would have to work out Darling. Wish they had a big enough farm so that you could be at home. But guess it is okay so long as you are living in Missouri. ha

So your father decided to bring his shop along -- the people here were glad to hear that he was. Were Emanuels there already? What did they have to say? Don't know will I get much done or not today. I just don't care what I do. I would feel more like working if you were here. You know, Honey, I have been thinking about husking corn this fall. Have to do something to make a little money, so that I can buy you a Christmas present. ha Well, I just can't think of anything more to write. My news box just ran empty all of a sudden. ha So will ring off for this time. With Love and Best wishes to you till we meet again.

Your true Loving sweetheart
Susie Ann Miller

Letters like these were very encouraging to Amos. He knew Susie felt just like he did. It seemed like time had come to a standstill. Two and a half months sure seemed like a long way off for him. He just had to see his sweetheart again. He would cling to her letters to get him through the days ahead.

Amos wrote to Susie . . .

Oct. 16, 1957

Dear Sweetheart,

Greetings of my purest Love to you. How does this find you in the boat of health? I am as usual, but miss you very much. Well, maybe I had better answer some of your questions you asked me in your letter. I wasn't expecting a letter from you today, but am glad the mail went through in two days. I felt more like working after I read your letter.

Yes, I was at Levi Hershberger's for dinner Sunday. Would have enjoyed myself better if you would have been there. No, I wasn't at the Singing because they didn't have one. So about a dozen of us boys went to Jonas's for the evening. Jonas asked me if my folks were back from Mo. I told him they were and that they had bought a place. My folks came home Sat. at 4 PM. I was glad they came home early. You asked what I'm doing? I finished up the henhouse on the inside. So tonight we spent over an hour catching and carrying pullets. There were a lot of them in the trees. We caught 206 of them, so guess most of them are in.

It was around 9 PM when we got done, so now I am writing your letter and it's 11 PM already.

No Darling, Emanuels haven't been over since the folks got home, so I don't know what they are going to say about it. You know, I don't like the idea of you husking corn, that's too hard work for you. Besides you might beat me in husking. ha I think I have answered all your questions for you. Guess I will stop for tonight, as I'm pretty sleepy, past bedtime for a little boy like me. ha Goodnight.

Good morning, hope you are feeling good this morning. I am feeling fine. It's almost 8 AM already and I should be at work. I have a few stripes on the outside of the henhouse to finish and a few doors. I need to go grind feed in PM and also make a creep for the pigs. Have so much work to get done before I come down to see you, but I guess it will make the time go faster. With best wishes and Love to you till we meet again.

Your true Loving Sweetheart

Amos Miller

Now it was back to work again for another week till Amos would get another letter. What helped him get through the week was re-reading Susie's letters until he received the next letter.

Amos was so thankful he had someone special to love and receive the same kind of love in return. Their "Bonding Love" grew stronger from not being able to see each other for months. It helped him to realize how much he loved Susie and that in time they could have a future together.

Amos received Susie's next letter very promptly.

Oct. 18, 1957

My Dearest Sweetheart,

Greetings of my Best Love to you. Received your ever so welcome letter just a few hours ago. I got the mail today. The first time I got the mail since I am home. You know we have 3/4 mile to get the mail. Our mailman goes about the same time yours does. Between 11:00 and 12:00 o'clock. Dad wanted me to go over to Chrissie Ropp's. It was exactly noon when I left, so of course, I was first at the mailbox.

How does this find you in health? I am just as usual except that I am happier since I have your letter. Wish I could have you instead. But guess the letters will have to do. The time would pass more quickly if you were here. It really seems like a long time since I have seen you last. It isn't two weeks yet but seems a lot longer. You know I am not one bit hungry when it is time to eat, and I always want something we don't have. They tell me it is zeitlang. Do you think so? I believe it is, because I think that is what my trouble is.

Now just who do you think I would have zeitlang for? Well it is you, darling, of course.

Boy you know I could still just kick myself that I didn't go back to Iowa with your folks. But maybe it is better this way. Don't you think so Honey? Would like to go with Dad's to Chillicothe tomorrow, but guess I had better stay at home, no more money than I have. Hope to get some from Ezras next week for sewing that I have done for her. I made little Susie Marie a little coat and does she ever look cute in it. You should just see it.

Yes, Honey we will have a little more than three miles when you will be living in Mo. That isn't very far is it? It won't take long to go those miles if we have your horse Sylvia. Do you think it will Darling? I have to tell you something right now. Maybe you know it by the time you read this letter and maybe you don't.

Wait a minute and don't rush me, then I'll get it on this paper. ha Yes Honey there was a woman here this afternoon. She said she is Ed Day's daughter, she wanted to know how she could get in touch with your Dad. She said they found a little flaw in the paperwork for the farm your folks bought.

Had to run for the stove because the milk was boiling over. Don't you smell it? Boy it really stinks.

I now think of a question I wanted to ask in my other letter. Was Emanuel there any day that your folks were down here? If he wasn't you really must have had long days all by yourself. With the little boys in school. Sure wished I was there to do your cooking. I really had to think about you a lot those days. I believe I was thinking about you all day long then. I still think about you all day long. There never goes one day by that I don't think of you. On the days you get my letter I think of you all day long Darling. I just can't help it my mind just roams back to Iowa where John U. Miller's live. Seems I just can't forget those people and I don't want to either. It is almost a wonder you don't see my mind up there sometimes as often as they are there.

Well Sweetie what did you do today? I started to cut my dark blue schatz and holsduch like that dress I made at your place. I also want to cut out my new gray dress one of these days.

Did you go to the wedding supper last night? Did you have to take a girl to the table or did you go with a bunch of boys? Sure wished I was there. Boy I can hardly bring it over myself that I am in Missouri instead of Iowa. Are you coming to Mo. before you move? Sure would be glad to see you come but now don't come just because I wrote this if you had not planned to. Not that I wouldn't be glad to see you come, but guess you would have more money then when you move. It is only a little over two months anymore.

How much corn do you have to husk? You know I don't think I'll work too hard if I go husk corn, and I don't think I'll beat you either, because I know you can husk a lot faster than I can. Gel? *[Right?]* It would go a little better if you were here to help me do it Sweetheart, don't you think? Well sheet is full and supper is ready, so will close with Luck, Love and best wishes to you.

From a true Loving Sweetheart,
Susie Ann Miller

After receiving a letter like this, Amos was on cloud nine again. He knew Susie's love for him was growing stronger and stronger. His love for her was also growing by leaps and bounds. He was glad they had the time frame they did to grow fonder of each other. It was hard to be apart, but Amos was sure it helped them so they would have a long future together—there would be fewer divorces if relationships were given time to grow. Amos's response to Susie's October 18 letter . . .

Oct. 21, 1957

My Dearest Loved Sweetheart,

Greetings of my Best Love to you. Received your ever so welcome letter today. I didn't know until tonight that I got a letter from you. We had gros gma today instead of Sunday. I was surprised to get a letter from you when I got the mail. I wasn't expecting one till Tues. or Wed., but you don't need to think that I wasn't glad to have one.

Boy I am a-telling you, I sure felt a lot happier after I read your letter. Boy I am a-telling you, I sure felt Blue before I read your letter. I was sitting all day in Church until I thought I couldn't sit any more. Where I was sitting was so tight I couldn't even put my legs straight out in front of me. There was a desk right in back of me, so that I had to sit straight up, so you can imagine how I felt when I got out of there. It was past 4:30 PM when Church let out. I felt like going to bed when I got home, but I didn't. The first thing I did was to read your letter. After that I felt like doing something.

Well, how are you feeling Sweetie? I am just feeling fine. My eyes quit hurting since I am at home. Anyway almost, so don't worry. All I want to hear is that you are feeling fine, would be sorry to hear otherwise. Well, you probably want to hear something else instead of my trouble. ha You will probably get tired of reading by the time you read this letter.

Well Darling, it could easy be that you have zeitlang if you don't feel like eating. But I can't see how you could have more of it than I do. I think I thought of you every hour today - - anyway when I wasn't sleeping. It's a wonder your ears didn't ring or did they? You know Sweetheart, sometimes I just don't feel like working at all. Wish you were here to watch me.

Maybe I'd feel more like working then. I don't think there's a single day gone by since you are home that I didn't think of you, Darling. Every time I come upstairs it seems like I should see you in that east room, but it's always empty.

But it seems that the days go faster than what I was afraid they would. Guess it makes a difference because I am busy working all the time, at least trying to be. Sure is a lot of work to do, seems like there is no end. I don't know which way is best. If you would have come back with my folks or stayed there. But I sure know I could use you up here. It sure seems lonely to be alone and nobody to hold in my arms to talk to.

Well, maybe I had better start to answer some more of your questions Darling, or else I'll have a book full of sheets for you to read. ha Well they called for supper but I am not a bit hungry.

Here I am again Honey, supper over with and it's almost 8 PM, so will try to finish your letter before I get too sleepy.

Well, what did you do last Sunday, Sweetheart? Some other boys and I were over at Kingsize. When we got there, Church had just let out. It was 7 PM already. Yes Sweetheart those three miles won't be long, wish I was that close to you now. I'm afraid you wouldn't be alone very long Darling. No, and I don't smell your milk that just boiled over, but wish I was there to smell it, then I would be close to you.

No, Emanuel wasn't here once while my folks were down there. My days almost felt like weeks to me. It's been quite cool lately. Guess I better start going down South to you, Sweetheart, where it's warm, how about it?

Yes, I was at that wedding that night. It was the longest and loneliest wedding night I ever went to. Sure wished you were here so I could of had a partner with me. Yes Darling I went to the table with a bunch of boys.

Well, Darling, I did say something to my folks about coming down to visit you before we move. Don't know if time will allow me the chance to come see you or not. Well, I haven't even started to husk corn yet, have 36 acres to husk if I ever get started. I want to get all the carpenter work done first you know, Sweetheart! If I had my own money, we'd be going to a wedding in Indiana, the one I told you about, they had told me to bring my steady.

No, Sweetheart we haven't heard anything from Andy yet. Mother wrote and told him that we bought a place in Jamesport, Mo. It's bedtime, so Goodnight Sweetheart.

Good morning, just got in from doing chores. Well, guess you will see Dad down there this week again, as they wanted to change the contract so the other people could draw their social security.

Well must get to work, with my Best Wishes and Love to you Sweetheart.

From your true Loving Sweetheart,
Amos J. Miller

Susie's response to his letter . . .

October 23, 1957

My Dearest Loved Sweetheart,

Greeting of my Best Love to you. Received your ever so welcome letter today. Thought I would write your letter right away so I can send it with your dad and save a stamp. ha Also thought that way you would get a letter in two days. ha. That way we will both get two letters this week. ha. Boy that will really be nice for once, gel Sweetheart!

Am happier since I read your letter. Seemed good to see your Dad this morning, but wished you were aw de bei *[along with]*. You know those doughnuts Barbara sent along with your dad? Well, I made them – so be sure and eat some of them. You know yesterday morning it was two weeks that I came home, but it seems much longer. It seems more like two months than two weeks.

I bet if you would have been expecting a letter from me on Monday, you could hardly have waited until Church was out, you would have been so anxious to get home, gel. Boy I know just how you would have felt.

Sweetheart, I am kind of anxious to start husking corn this fall. Well, everybody else is going to bed so guess I'll go too. So goodnight and sweet dreams. I'll probably see you in my dreams because I usually do.

Good morning, it's 7AM and really cold this morning. Well, sweetheart, what will you do today? Hope it isn't too cold up there if you have to work on that porch. Did you decide already which day you will have your sale? Wish I was there to help you get ready for the sale and also get ready to move. Wish I was going to Iowa with your dad, but can't, so we will have to do the next best - which is writing.

Boy, you know I sure wished I was in that wedding. Then you wouldn't have had to sit beside all those girls. But guess as long as you got through the wedding without being hurt it is okay. Must finish up as your dad is ready to go.

With Love Luck and Best Wishes from

Your True Loving Sweetheart,
Susie Ann Miller

Amos kept busy helping to get ready for the sale and the move to Missouri. He was counting the days now—he couldn't wait to see Susie again. Her letters kept him going. It was his turn to write, so that evening in his room, Amos wrote to his Sweetheart.

Chapter 20

# Love Continues to Grow

Oct. 25, 1957

My Dearest Loved Sweetheart,

Greetings of my Best Love to you. Received your welcome letter around 2 PM yesterday, was sure glad to get it. Was hoping I'd see you instead of a letter. But guess letters will do as long as I have a True Love to write to, like you Sweetheart.

Yes, last night I was at Hazleton to get Dad. It was 20 degrees and cold wind. Took my horse and the top buggy, but it was still cold. I got there at 12 midnight. I wanted to be a few minutes early so Dad didn't have to wait in the cold. I waited for quite a while, no bus, so I looked at the time and it was 1:40 a.m. already -- and no bus. So I told myself I'll wait till 2 a.m. and go home. About that time, the bus came.

Well, it's 8:30 a.m. already and I just started to write your letter. Would have written your letter last night but it was 2:30 a.m. this morning when I finished reading your letter.

Well, Darling, yesterday I finished the porch, all except the door. Sweetheart, your doughnuts sure were good this morning, wish you could have been here to share them with me.

Well, those cold sores better go away, or I might have to come down there and kiss them away. No, I didn't get tired of reading about your troubles, just be sure you share them with me. I want to know how you feel, no matter what it is, I want you to share it with me.

I bet your afternoon went kind of slow when you were waiting on my letter. No, we haven't decided which day we will have sale, probably some time in December. Yes, guess it was okay that I made it through that wedding without getting hurt, but it sure wasn't enjoyable without you being there.

Well, I should get to work -- it's 9 AM already. With my Best Wishes and Love to you sweetheart.

From a true Loving Sweetheart,
Amos Miller

Susie was so lonesome for Amos. If only she could talk to someone about it, but her parents didn't seem to want to hear about her "silly notions."

She would start a letter for Amos tonight and then maybe she would feel better.

Oct. 26, 1957

Dearest Loved One,

Greetings of Love to you. How does this find you in health? I am just as usual except a little sleepy. I received your ever so welcome letter today. Was I ever glad to see that letter. It sure seemed long since I had sent your letter with your dad. Don't know, maybe I am just kindish *[silly]* that the time seems so long for me. But the days just go by so slow. They go much slower than they did when I was in Indiana. And of course, lots slower than when I was in Iowa. I thought I would start your letter tonight so I would have more time.

Guess I'll go home after Church tomorrow evening. Will not be in the Singing. Don't know will I get the evening brought around or not. Boy, last Sunday evening sure was a lonesome one. I missed you just as much then as I did the first Sunday evening. You know last Sunday evening I had a short date with little Susie Marie. ha Her little kisses were really sweet but not as sweet as yours, that you also gave me when I was there. Boy, Sweetheart you know it was really hard to see your dad go home Thursday and to think I couldn't go with him. I said something to Mother about going with him but she said don't be so silly. Whenever I say something about going to Iowa they just scold me and tell me not to be so silly. That is one thing that makes it so hard for me and why I get zeitlang. I can't talk to anybody about a little this and that without them telling me to stop talking about you. So maybe now you know why I miss you and even your mom and dad so much. Goodnight Sweetheart.

But please, Darling don't let that make a difference. Because it would just simply break my heart if you would stop on me now. I will just not say anything about it anymore. So hope you won't be thinking bad about me to write you this, because I have to tell someone my troubles.

This is now Sunday evening about 8 PM. Didn't go to the Singing because I don't care to go if you aren't here. Oh, it is so lonesome here without you. If I wasn't supposed to do some sewing for Barbara, I don't know would I be here or not. Yes, Sweetheart a wedding was published today. Joe Gingerich and Lydia Detwiler. But it isn't going to be fun to go to the wedding without you.

The others are eating supper, but I am not a bit hungry. I'm full of lovesick and zeitlang for you Darling. Oh, why can't it be that we can be together. Well guess I might just as well forget it because it can't be done but de zeit *[maybe some day]*. Am hoping and praying for that time to come.

Oh, I am so tired of working out. I just don't know what I am going to do yet. Wish I could start husking corn next week, but doubt that I can. Sure was glad to hear you liked those doughnuts. Because I didn't know what else to send to you. Your Dad bought some dates, then he left some for me. Said maybe those will help a little. They helped some, but not too much. You know, sometimes it does more good to talk to ourselves than we realize. You didn't ask very many questions. Don't know will my sheet get full or not. Hope so though because I would like to have some more fat letters from you -- like the one was that I got last Wednesday.

Yes Darling, I think it would help if you would come and kiss my cold sore, because it is still there. I think that is what it is waiting for. Wish I was there with you to spend the evening.

Yes, I dreamed about you the last three nights. That one night we were having a date. I just saw you as plain as if you would have been here and it had been in the daytime. But oh how mistaken when I woke up and it was just a dream. Sheet is full. Wishing you luck.

Love and Best wishes from a true Lover,
Susie Ann Miller

There! Now Susie felt better. She knew Amos would understand her feelings. Was Amos having zeitlang like she was? Susie was counting the days until the Millers would move to their district.

Amos answered Susie's letter promptly.

Oct. 30, 1957

Dearest Loved One,

Greetings of Love to you Sweetheart. How does this find you in health? For me, I am okay, but a little happier since I got your letter. I sure was watching and watching for the mailman today.

Well, I don't think you are kindish that the time seems to go slow for you, because it does for me too. I am just glad to hear that you get zeitlung. I wouldn't think you Loved me very much if you didn't, don't you think so? Well, I hope I can cheer you up a little until you are done reading this letter.

Well, Sweetheart, I don't feel a bit bad for how you wrote that they scold you if you say something about coming up here. And Sweetheart, you don't need to worry that I'll ever, ever stop Loving you, because I just couldn't, I Love you too much. I am just glad you wrote something about it, so I know how they are treating you.

It's 12:30 PM and I didn't eat dinner yet. Guess I will have to fix my own dinner as I am by myself. Mom and Dad went to Oelwein today. I am not a bit hungry so that's why I started to write your letter. Bet you couldn't guess why I am writing your letter right away!

Well, I have some good news for you Sweetheart. thought if I wrote your letter right away it would seem like I am telling it to you. Well anyway, here it goes, hope you call it good news. I expect to leave Iowa next Tuesday, November 5 for Jamesport, Mo., so you know what that means. I will be seeing you in a week from today. Won't that be wonderful to see each other again Sweetheart?

Now don't feel that I am coming because of the way you wrote. I was going to come before I received your letter. I knew last Sunday night already that there was supposed to be a wedding down there. Fred's Dan told me. He told me that he was going to go down there for the wedding, and he wanted me to go along. I told him I had to ask my folks first, and I would let him know next Sunday. Dan offered to give me $20 if I go along. He said I could pay him back sometime later.

So Sweetie, don't be looking too much for me on Wednesday in case we change plans and come on Thursday. Our plans now are to come on Wednesday, thought I'd let you know so you won't be disappointed if we didn't get there on Wednesday. Well, maybe I should get back to work. It is almost 1 PM already. Hope you will feel better when you get done reading my letter, will finish writing tonight.

Here I am again, just got done eating supper. It's after 7 PM so guess I will have plenty of time to write before I get too sleepy. Guess I had better start catching up with my sleep so I can stay awake to see you. I am sure I will lose some sleep when I get down there, don't you think so Sweetheart? Was sorry to hear about your troubles, but I am sure they will go away when I get down there, think so Darling?

Well Sweetheart, you aren't the only one that is full of Lovesick because I am full of it, that I just feel like not working. Sometimes I am thinking so much of you that I forget what I am doing. Like today I went up to the toolshed to get some staples to put on the netting on the chicken house door. Then when I got back to the henhouse I happened to think that I forgot the netting. I had just thrown it outside the shed to take it along down, so I had to go back up and get the netting. This wasn't the first time I forgot something. Just seems like I am daydreaming all the time, maybe it will help stop the dreaming once I get down there.

Well Honey, I got that washhouse finished yesterday and started to finish the chicken house. Now I have to fix the toolshed and a little work on the corn crib, then I should be ready to start husking corn.

Are you working at Ezra's right now? Hope so because I was planning to go there for breakfast the morning I come down there. Well Sweetheart, maybe your dreams can come true when I get down there Wed. Expecting to see you happy as a lark when I get there. I bet you were surprised when you read my letter. Well, I could have not written anything about me coming and then surprise you, but I thought you would want to know that I was coming - - or at least I would have wanted to know if you were coming to see me. I was afraid I would surprise you too much so that you wouldn't enjoy yourself if I didn't let you know before I came.

Well, I bet you felt a lot better after you read my letter. But the time probably will seem long for you until I come, it sure seems a long ways off for me anyway.

Good morning. How are you feeling this morning? I feel okay but a little sleepy. It's 7 AM and I didn't have breakfast yet. Breakfast wasn't ready when I came in from doing chores, so thought I would write some before breakfast.

Oh yes, Mother told me to tell you to get a wedding present for the wedding if you are invited, then if I am invited, I will pay for half. If this is okay with you Darling? You will probably get tired of reading this big letter. Anyway I hope talking will go better than writing when I get down there. It will probably seem like a dream to you until you see me coming. Think so Sweetheart? It seems like a dream to me that I am going down there to see you finally. Seems the days go twice as slow since I found out that I am going to come down there to see you. This is probably the last letter you will get from me before I see you Sweetheart. But I am expecting a big fat letter from you yet before I see you Darling. You know, I can hardly wait until Sunday is past - - seems like it is a long ways off. You know Sweetheart, I think this is the longest letter I ever wrote you. But maybe you will feel better after you are done reading all of my scribbling. Well, I should be getting to work Sweetie. So Long Sweetheart. Good Luck and Best wishes and Love to you till we meet again. Hope to see you soon.

From a true Loving Sweetheart,
Amos Miller

Susie's response to Amos's October 30th letter . . .

Nov. 1, 1957

My Dearest Sweetheart,

Greeting of purest Love to you. Received your wonderful and ever so welcome letter about an hour ago. The time really seemed long since your last letter. Of course it will be a week tomorrow. But am just glad I get them as quick as I do.

Wonder how you are feeling by now? I am just as usual except a lot happier since I read your letter. Boy was I surprised when I found out that you are coming next week. But you know it seems a little ways off yet. But am really tickled to have you come. I could just have jumped up and down for joy when I read it. ha

What are you all doing? I haven't been doing very much and still I was busy most of the time. Wednesday forenoon I made a light green Sunday shirt for Ezra. Yesterday I seamed 20 diapers for Barbara. Had an everyday shirt to make for Ezra but the thread got all so guess I'll have to find something else to do. I helped Dad's move the turkeys in AM and helped Mom peel walnuts this afternoon. Sadie is now helping her. I have also been sewing on my tea towels in the evenings after supper.

I have something else to tell you and maybe show you when you come. I also will have a surprise for you. ha You don't know how tickled and pleased I was to get such a big letter from you. And I never get tired of reading them. I wouldn't get tired reading them if you wrote a whole tablet full. You know there isn't any kind of letter I like to get better than great big fat ones. But if somebody doesn't send me any like those, I don't get mad because I don't always send some like that. ha

Boy Sweetheart, I am just so tickled and overjoyed about you coming that I can hardly keep my mind on my letter writing. I just keep thinking how happy I will be when you are here. I hope you will want to go see your home sometime when you are here. Because I would also like to see it sometime. Guess Mom, Sadie, and I will go out to Ezra's tomorrow to help Barbara can her pears. I will not be working at Ezra's next week that I know of but intend to be there. I will tell Barbara tomorrow that you are coming. Then I will tell her to have Ezra come after me Monday evening. Then I can do her washing Tuesday and stay until Wednesday sometime, then you can go home with me. Levi just now came home from school. Don't know what time it is. Guess I'll go see. Maybe I will know more to write after supper. So Long Sweetheart.

Hi Darling. This is now schund *[already]* after supper. Don't know how much I'll get written. Boy I am just so happy to have you come that I can hardly wait until Wednesday morning. Wish you would come on Tuesday morning. I guess Wednesday morning is aw -- it's OK. I am just glad you can come on Wednesday morning. Anyway, you didn't write how long you are staying. Am really gwunnerich *[curious]*. Hope you will stay over Sunday.

Boy, I know now that I will enjoy myself at the wedding if you are here. Guess I'll have to go make some more fire. We have to cook our drinking water so we can drink it. It tastes so bad if we don't cook it. The fire is now made and I am now settled to finish this letter. Guess I'll have to read your letter so that I can answer your questions.

Yes, I suppose it would be so, Darling. If I didn't get zeitlung for you, I probably wouldn't Love you very much. But I sure hope you do know that I Love you very much. Because I just can not see how I could do without you. And I am also glad to hear that you love me enough to not stop even if you know all of my troubles. Yes Honey, I know that my parents aren't like yours are, but I Love them just the same. Because I don't think I could do without them unless I just had to. But maybe things will change when you are living here. I hope you will also write your troubles. Although I know you don't have any troubles like I have. I feel I should also know yours if you have any. What did you eat for dinner the day you started my letter? It is none of my business but just wondered. ha Hope you ate enough so that you didn't go hungry. Boy I tell you, it sure was good news to hear that you are coming. The rest of this day has gone a little faster already. But no telling about the other days. Yes Sweetheart, that will be about the most wonderful thing that has happened for us so far yet.

I didn't expect you to come just because I wrote what I did but I just thought I would probably feel better if I told you. You know Sweetheart that really was nice of Dan to give you $20 to come. We can at least have one good word for him, can't we Sweetie?

I am caught up with my sleep now mol *[finally]* because the last few nights I woke up and was awake for a while. Guess I'll have to sleep a lot more so that I won't be so sleepy when you come. Yes, I believe you will lose some sleep when you come. At least I hope so. I am figuring so and hope you are too. You know there are only five more sheets of this stationery left. There are still a few envelopes left, but I will just use my tablet then.

I hope my troubles will all leave me when you come. Some of them have left me already, just since I have read your letter. I also feel more like singing.

Glad to hear that you have all the buildings fixed. About how long do you think it will take you to get the corn husked? Do you have to do it alone?

You don't have to worry and think that I won't be happy as a lark Wednesday morning. But you had better not wait until Thursday because that would be the morning of the wedding. I sure am glad you wrote me that you are coming. Because it was a big enough surprise the way it was. It would have been a bigger surprise if I wouldn't have known it until I would have seen you. Believe me, I really was surprised. I wasn't one bit tired of reading your letter. I was just glad to have such a big one to read. I know talking will go better. It does almost seem like a dream. It is bedtime. Wishing you Luck, Love and Best wishes till we meet again.

From a true Loving Sweetheart,
Susie Ann Miller

After Susie and Amos had shared their true feelings so deeply in the longest letters they had ever written, they both knew they wanted to spend the rest of their lives together. Amos was a little nervous, but he wanted to "pop the Big Question" when he got to Missouri. Can you blame him?

Chapter 21

# Bonds of Purest Love

The day finally arrived for Amos to start his trip to Missouri to see his sweetheart. It was still like a dream to him that he was actually going to see his true love . . . the one he was so homesick for. The past days had been very long for both of them.

The bus pulled in on time. After the bus started to move, Amos finally fully realized he was on his way.

Amos knew he had to change buses in Des Moines, Iowa, but that didn't bother him. This was his first trip by himself away from home. He had only one thing in mind. He would get to hold and cherish Susie his loved one who had taken his heart and loved it like her own.

He had many thoughts while riding the bus on the way down to Missouri. How should he greet his lovely Susie? Should he just run and hug her and not care who sees them? Well they were taught not to kiss in public and not to show too much affection for everyone to see. But his heart yearned so much for Susie, he just didn't know what to expect from himself. Then again, what would Susie think? Would she want him to hug and kiss her right away or wait till they were by themselves?

Then he started to recall her letter to him when she found out he was coming to see her. She greeted his letter with purest love, and said she was glad and happier since reading his letter. Susie had replied that she was overjoyed, pleased, surprised, and tickled so much that she could have just jumped up and down for joy. Susie also reminded Amos that she loved him very much and couldn't do without him. She said she was glad that he loved her very much and that she felt like singing since she read his letter. Most of all, this is the most wonderful thing that has happened to them—they will be together again. Susie had a surprise for Amos when he got there.

After recapping all these facts, why should Amos have any fear of how he would act when he met her? Susie will probably act and respond the same as he and any homesick lovers would! After thinking all this over in his mind, Amos asked himself, "What are you worried about?" Then Amos also had in mind that big question, "Will you marry me?" He was pretty sure she would after sharing with him how she loved him, but he still had butterflies.

When Amos arrived at Ezra's, Susie was there, anxiously waiting. Susie was smiling ear to ear. He could tell she really wanted to hold him and he wanted to hug and hold her. Susie later told Amos that she felt like running out and hugging him no matter who might see them.

After Amos's short greeting with Barbara and the little girls, Susie took his hand said, "Come with me." After hugging each other in private, things were a lot better. They just held each other for quite a while, no words were needed to express how they felt. That was one of the most rejoicing moments in their life. Their love had bonded them together in a very real way. Then the thought occurred to Amos about the big question, "When is the right time to ask?" Well, he finally thought it would be better to wait till later on when they were off cloud nine. Then it occurred to him that he was five years younger than Susie, would that make a difference to her? Well those butterflies jumped around a little again. Then he thought he would just wait till a little later on—maybe they will be talking about how they feel about each other. Maybe he can kind of blend the question in as they share their love with each other.

Later the next evening, things were going quite well and Amos felt more sure of himself. Then it happened—Susie showed him the surprise she had mentioned in her letter. She showed him a sample of a nice dark navy blue material and asked Amos if he liked it. He said he liked it very much. Then Susie asked if he thought that would make a nice wedding dress some day. Amos said he thought it would. That put Amos at ease and he just knew this would be the right time to ask that "Big Question" and that Susie would say yes.

So here goes, "Susie, would you marry me?" He didn't have to wait long for his answer—which was "Yes." Amos was very thankful for her showing that material sample and giving him the courage to ask her to marry him.

From then on, they had plenty of things to discuss. "When do we want to set the date?" "What will my folks say?" "I am only eighteen, what will your parents say?" Then they had to ask themselves, "Do we think they will approve because of the length of time it would be to the date of the wedding? Today is November 6, 1957 and the wedding will be planned for October 23, 1958." By that time Amos would be nineteen years old. And before they got married Amos would have to be baptized and join the Church. He would have to also have communion once before they got married. So by having to do all this, they came up with the date of October 23, 1958.

It is a tradition of the Amish to keep things like this a secret until closer to the wedding event. So Amos and Susie decided to tell only their folks and none of their brothers and sisters at this early stage. But they thought it best to even wait for a while before they told their folks.

They had a very good enjoyable time for those five days, but Amos needed to go home. He had to get his corn husked and get ready for the sale so he and the family could move to Missouri.

The morning parting was very hard for both of them, but through their love they made it by thinking of their future. They both agreed if they can make it for another two months, they will have time together every week once Amos moved to Missouri—but that sure seemed far away yet. They had the hope of living the rest of their lives together and those thoughts helped them a lot too. They had a commitment to each other—they wanted to spend their lives together. This was a true bond of love they could cling to.

Amos wrote a card to Susie on the way home, when he got into Des Moines.

Nov. 11, 1957

Hi Honey,

I am sitting here in Des Moines waiting on my bus, it's around 6 PM. I have about an hour's wait, feeling OK.

Wonder how you are feeling tonight? I'll write you a letter when I get home, thought this card would reach you quicker.

A loving friend,
Amos Miller

Amos arrived home okay, but felt very lonely. His first letter to Susie after he got home . . .

Nov. 12, 1957

Dearest loved Sweetheart,

Greeting of my best love to you. How does this find you feeling this morning? For me, well, I'm feeling about as good as can be expected.

Well, you know what? I made it home okay last night. When I got off at Hazleton there was a Waterloo worker who got off too. So I had him take me home. You probably were sleeping and didn't find it out anyway. ha It was 2 AM when I got home.

Sweetheart it is 9:30 AM already, and I just started to write your letter. Boy Sweetheart, it sure seems lonesome not having you around this morning, but guess it was about time to come home. When I got here, they were all sick in bed with the flu. The neighbors did the chores for them a couple of times. Dad got sick the next day after I left for Mo.

You know, Sweetheart, I don't know if you can read my scribbling this morning or not? Seems like my hand doesn't want to write nice this morning.

I should hurry and finish this letter as I need to go to Hazleton to get some coal, as they pretty near burned up all the wood I had on hand. I want to go in time so I can catch the 1:00 PM bus to Independence. Want to get a treatment on my neck and back. You know sweetie, I just can't think of much to write this morning. Guess my head's a little sleepy. ha

When I got home, my folks didn't even know that Ezra's had a little baby or that I was sick. They just figured I was sick or else I would have come home sooner. They said Vatures, Ezra's neighbors, didn't even say anything about it when they called.

Guess Mother is writing Ezras a letter this morning too. She said not to seal my letter right away so she can put hers in too.

So guess I'll put her letter in with mine. ha Hey, Sweetheart, when that dress material comes, let me know, not that I have to know but would like to. Guess it's just as much mine as yours—someday. Think so Sweetheart? Well I had better get busy so I get to town on time. Hope to get a big fat letter from you Sat. and let me know any of your troubles and news. With my best wishes and love to you.

A true loving sweetheart,
Amos J. Miller

Susie's response to Amos's letter of November 12, 1957.

Nov. 13, 1957

Dearest loved Sweetheart,

Received your ever so welcome letter today. Also the card that you wrote in Des Moines. Wonder how you are by now? I am feeling better again but still not okay. Monday noon I started getting sick. So by evening I went home, then Sadie came out to Ezra's. Felt some better today, so Mom thought I could go back to Ezra's again. Didn't get your letter until I got to Ezra's around 3 PM. Have quite a bit headache yet, but hope I'll be better by morning.

You know Sweetheart, I just have to tell you that my dress material came today. I want to put in a pretty big sample of it so that you can really see it. You can show your folks if you want to. Did you tell them already what we planned? I haven't told any of my sisters or brothers, and I don't intend to yet for the time being. I just thought we and both our folks can keep it a secret yet for a while. There is something else I just have to tell you, Darling. Today I was in to see Mr. Spillman at the Jamesport Bank. I asked him about borrowing some money to buy two sows. He said he would loan me the money. So sometime now before long I want to go to some town to buy them. Of course, I'll let Dad do the bidding to buy them.

I wouldn't have much money left from the spring pigs but the sows would be paid for then. But after the fall pigs would be sold, we could have that money then, and we would also have the sows whenever we got started for ourselves. We could use the money we get from the fall pigs for the wedding expenses.

Just tell me exactly how you feel about it all honey. I thought it would be good if both our folks knew about our wedding plans, so my folks have plenty of time if they want to add onto the house. They had been talking about adding a porch on the east side and also on the south side. It may look quite a bit different around here by the time we want to be having a wedding. Will have more room then so that we can have a big wedding too.

I have now planned to be in Iowa for Christmas and your sale. I want to ask Will Schrock's Lydia if she wants to go with me. If she doesn't, I'll just go by myself. I am not afraid to go by myself. Anyway not if I go on the bus. I have gone that way often enough already that I am not afraid to go by myself. Yes Sweetie, I'll be seeing you again Friday or Saturday in five weeks. That seems quite a ways off yet but it will be here before we know it. Especially after I get to husking corn. I know I am forgetting about half the things I wanted to write. Well, guess I'll read your letter and see what questions you asked. Maybe I will think of all the other things I wanted to write yet.

Sure will be tickled to see your folks if they come next week. Will help make the week shorter. But wish it was you that was coming again. Guess it will do now till I come up there to Iowa.

Boy I was sure glad to hear you got home all right. Sure thought a lot about you that day. Woke up once during the night, and I just wondered if you were at home already or not. Don't know what time it was. But you weren't gone more than one hour until I missed you so much, I could have cried. I tell you it is no wonder I missed you. Every time I needed water you were right there to get it. And whenever dishwashing time came, you were always there to dry the dishes for me. Boy the whole afternoon was just so lonesome. Several times I couldn't help it, I just had to let the tears roll because I missed you so much. Well, I better write something else or you will think I am really silly.

Yes, I reckon it was time you did go home. If they were all in bed with the flu they needed you and I guess I would miss you all the more if you would have stayed longer. But anyway, I figure the time is coming when we can be together all the time and won't have to part until death parts us. But let's not think of that already. Let us just be happy and think of the time coming. I hope your back feels a lot better now. What did your folks say that you didn't come home sooner? Hope they didn't care if you were sick which I doubt that they did. Yes I read the letter that your mother sent along for Ezras. You didn't use very many sheets in writing but what you did write sure meant a lot to me. Sweetheart, I was kind of surprised that I got so much on paper that I have, but guess I just knew more to write than I thought I did. Seems like I should know something more to write, but I just can't think of anything more. So will close wishing you God's richest blessing. God be with you till we meet again.

From a true loving sweetheart,
Susie Ann Miller

Amos's response to Susie's letter of November 13.

Nov. 17, 1957

Dearest loved Sweetheart,

Greetings of my best love to you. How does this find you in the line of health? For me I am feeling okay except sometimes I get a little coughing spell.

I was sorry to hear that you got sick too after I left you. Sweetheart, you know there would have been somebody there to take care of you if I could have been there. I can hardly stand it that I am not down there to take care of you now when you are sick. I am sure you would get better quicker if I was there to take care of you, don't you think so Sweetheart?

Well, maybe I better change the subject to make you feel better. Last night I told my folks what we were planning for our wedding. Mother said it's just what I thought you would say. So guess they weren't surprised too much. Sweetheart don't think you're silly for crying after I left. I know just how you felt. And don't feel bad for writing it. It kind of made me feel good to know that you loved me so much that you could hardly keep the tears away. But try to cheer up a little until I see you at Christmas, Sweetheart.

It's 9:30 AM already, I didn't go to Church because I stayed home to take care of Joni. It was okay with me that way I could write your letter and also get some sleep. ha I also have my cousin's letter to write sometime today. Sure wish you were here to spend the day with me.

Say Sweetheart about you coming by yourself, I don't like it that you will come by yourself, but guess it's okay. I will meet you at Hazleton when you come regardless how the weather is. It isn't that I don't want you to come, but usually there's nothing but men on that Waterloo bus. When I went home that way, there were only two girls on the bus.

Sweetheart, if you want to know how much it costs to come to Iowa, here is a list. From Jamesport to Winston $.66 – from there to Des Moines $3.37 – from Des Moines to Waterloo $3.36 – from Waterloo to Hazleton $1.05. That's a total of $8.44 for fares.

Yes, my folks are coming down this week. Sure will be lonesome to be all alone again. But guess I'll pull through as long as you are coming up for Christmas. Well, my back and eyes are feeling better though I didn't go get a treatment like I was going to. Dad gave me three foot treatments, three nights in a row and I feel better. And my folks didn't have much to say that I didn't come home sooner. They figured I might be sick too.

Sweetheart, don't say you were hard on me when I was down there because you weren't. Guess you must have got the flu from me. Wish I would have been there to take care of you. Yes, that would be making pretty good money for you if you can husk that much corn. Do you have to scoop the corn off or do you have an elevator to unload it? Hope you don't have to scoop it off because that's too hard of work for you.

Anyway, Sweetheart, we can expect to be together someday and enjoy ourselves then you won't have to work so hard. I am just as anxious as you are to be together and have a happy life together. Anyway I hope you still feel that way Sweetheart? I am going to treat you just the way I told you when I was down there, hope you haven't forgotten what all I told you.

About buying those sows, I felt you were doing pretty good. You made me feel that I have a nice girl that I can depend on all the time - - at least I don't know where I could get a better one. I am just glad you are mine, I wouldn't want anyone else even if I could get a dozen of them. I just want you to know that I never want to be away from you.

Seems like I can't write so nice and understanding letters as you can Sweetheart. Seems like you are always understanding, no matter what I ask of you. Well, Sweetheart, what are you doing these days? For me I have plenty to do. Friday I took the big engine apart and fixed it so I could grind some corncobs for the chicken house. I get mixed up on my speaking sometimes, so guess you can see how dumb I am, so you know before you marry me. ha

Boy, Sweetheart, I sure wish I was down there with you today. Seems like a couple of weeks since I saw you but it's only a week tomorrow. You know, you just can't realize how I feel not having you close by my side. And tonight Sweetheart, my arms are going to be oh so empty and the evening so long. But Sweetheart, you don't need to think that I don't think of you even if you aren't here in my arms. Well I need to go let the cattle out, maybe I can finish this in the morning.

Good morning, Sweetheart, how are you feeling? Hope fine, I am feeling fine but a little cold. We had three inches of snow this morning. Well, what did you do last night? I was at the Singing but didn't have any fun there. Wonder if it snowed down there or if you are husking corn? I want to take the rest of the cobs out of the corn crib and put them in the brooder house. I need to get the cribs ready for corn. Mother just called and said she is ready to have her wash water carried, so I had better put a stopper to this letter.

Wishing you God's richest blessings. Love, luck, and best wishes and God be with you till we meet again.

From your true loving sweetheart,
Amos J. Miller

Susie's response to Amos's November 13 letter.

Nov. 20,1957

Dearest loved Sweetheart,

Greetings of purest love to you. I received your ever, ever so welcome letter just a little while ago. I went to the mailbox and got it myself. Had to go through mud but I didn't care. I would go through almost anything for a letter from you. I was out to the mailbox yesterday and I was really disappointed that there wasn't any letter there. But guess it just happened that your letter didn't go through in two days this time. I suppose you will be looking for a letter on Friday, and there won't be any there for you. I know just how you will feel then, but hope you will be cheered up by Saturday.

Well, I wonder how you are by the time this reaches you? Hope sailing in the boat of good health. As for me I'm feeling fine again. Got over the flu okay which I am glad for. I know that you would have taken care of me if you would have been here. But you weren't here so I just had to take care of myself.

Your folks didn't care then that we have planned to marry? Did you tell them that I have planned to be there over Christmas? Glad to hear that they don't care, aren't you? So you don't think I was silly for crying after you left. It sure makes me feel good to know that.

You know Sweetheart it seems like two weeks already that you left. But the last few days passed kind of quickly, so hope the rest of the days pass quickly too.

Yes, I sure wished I was with you on Sunday because the day was a little long for me too. Of course, I was at Ezra's. My folks, Sadie, and Levi were there for dinner. Felty Lambrights were there in the afternoon. So the day wasn't too awful long. I went home with my folks in the evening, and Sadie stayed there to do the washing on Monday. Sure was glad to go home again for a change. Hope the day wasn't too awful long for you.

Did you get your cousin's letter written? Hope so, anyway I know you got mine written. I am glad you sent me the rates, but I don't think I'll go that way because it is me kinda of a druvel*[concern]* there in Waterloo to go on the workers' bus. I was thinking about starting in Trenton Monday evening the 16th of December. Go from Trenton to south Washington. Have my sister meet me there then go to Iowa City the next day about 11:00 AM. go on the bus and be in Hazleton at 4:00 PM Tuesday. That way I wouldn't have to wait so long in Des Moines, and I wouldn't have to go on the workers' bus. I would of course have to wait at my sister's place, but I would rather wait there than at Des Moines. So you won't have to worry about me on the worker's bus. So there will be only four weeks until I'll be seeing you again. That is if everything goes all right. Of course by the time you get this letter it will be only about three more weeks. You know, next week I am going to send a letter for you on Wednesday so that you get it on Saturday. Of course that would be the day that I would be supposed to send one for you but just thought in case I didn't get yours until Wednesday, then you would still get yours the right time.

How long will your folks stay? Mrs. Ed Day told my folks they were coming Saturday. Suppose they will start Friday evening gel? Anyway I hope your days won't be too long when they are gone.

I am really glad your father is a doctor that way it won't cost you so much whenever one of you get sick. I have seen a book like that already about how to treat the feet. I have had foot treatments too already and I know they help a lot.

Am glad your folks felt the way they did about you not coming home sooner because I was just afraid they might not like it.

You weren't too hard on me either when you were here because I got through okay. I'd rather have got the flu from you than anybody else, don't you think so Sweetheart?

No, I don't have to scoop the corn but I haven't started to pick any yet either. Am kind of anxious to get at it. Because I haven't got too much time. No, I wouldn't get mad at you if you were here and would scoop that corn for me. I would just be glad if you were here to do it for me.

Yes, Sweetheart, it sure is a pleasure and past time to be thinking that some day we can have a happy life together. I sure feel that way yet Sweetheart. I don't think I will ever forget what all you said when you were here.

I do not think you are silly to write about me like you did because I feel the same way about you. I just thought about buying those sows. It would help me make money and I wouldn't have to work out all the time.

Oh yes, Sweetheart, there was a man here Sunday evening that wanted a maid. They said they would give me $21 a week, but I didn't go because it was pretty far from here and I was thinking about getting my letters. Maybe I should have gone but mol anyway I didn't. Hope you don't think bad of me because I am bound to pick corn.

Don't feel bad about your letters because yours are just as nice and understanding as mine are. Because you are just as understanding as I am, no matter what I ask you. I have to get fire started in the kitchen, will be back before long.

I am back again. Sadie and Levi just now finished milking. Supper isn't quite ready yet. Thought I could scribble a few lines yet before supper. It is 6 PM. I went with Mother back to the turkeys. Sure wish they were sold so that they would have some more money and not so much work. Br-r-r-r-r, I tell you it is really cold here in Missouri. It isn't any wonder that we had some snow here Monday. If you had three inches of snow Monday morning, the snow that we had here on Monday was probably just the top snow blowing down here from up there in Iowa. ha Anyway it snowed Monday forenoon and part time in the afternoon.

Mother just now took a sheet of the letter that I am writing to you and is reading it. Sadie was going to read it too so I told her she doesn't have to read it. Now she is mad at me. But anyway I don't care if she is because I don't want her to read this letter. Supper is ready so guess I'll stop again for now. Why don't you come and help eat?

Supper is past and dishes washed. It is just 7:00 PM. Hope I can finish this tonight. Guess if I can't I'll just finish in the morning.

What are you all doing schund vile *[the last while]*? Do you have the tool shed roof schund done? Wonder if you started to pick corn already or are you just fixing the corn crib? I made myself a new Sunday slip, and I cut my new gray dress. The one I got at Jonas Bontrager's. Would like to have it finished to wear Sunday if it isn't muddy. Of course I'll have to get some gray thread yet sometime. Guess if Mom and Dad go to Jamesport tomorrow I'll let them get some. I started to piece a quilt but I decided to wait until we are going for ourselves then maybe someday I can have a quilting.

I don't think I'll get tired of your beard when you start joining church because you won't have to let your beard grow here until you are published to be married. I know you will like that a lot better. Don't you think you will? And don't think you are asking silly questions. Just ask any questions you want to and I'll try my best to answer them.

No, Sweetheart, you know I wouldn't want you to be in a bunch of boys like those Buck Co boys were that were here. I don't think it was very nice of them to act like they did. I really think they should be ashamed of themselves.

I missed you Sunday night and I do every night but I also again think we will be seeing each other at Christmas if nothing happens. That also helps make the time a little shorter.

The ground is frozen here too. But now is the time to go corn picking when it is frozen then it won't be muddy. Sure wish I was there to see all that snow but maybe some day when I am there you will have more than three inches of snow.

Well I just read your letter again, so I suppose you are picking corn by now. Wish I was there to help you. So Abe Bontrager is Bishop, wonder if they are coming now or not. They wanted to come down to see their daughter Susie now if she is taken back into church. Suppose it will be awhile until they will come now.

No I wasn't going to make my dress yet for a while. I may not get it made until I just need it. ha I just put it away and thought I would forget about it for de zeit *[the time being]*. Yes, Sweetheart, it is all right with me to just keep still about it. I thought I wouldn't tell until next summer sometime and maybe not until next fall. It just depends on what they write. If they would plan to come before I would of course write them to wait until then, but I also think it is best to just not tell for now.

The others are getting ready to go to bed, it is just 8:00 PM and I am not very sleepy, but maybe I can sleep anyway if I go to bed. Well goodnight, - sweet dreams.

This is now Thursday morning. It is colder again, but not too awful cold. It is almost 7:00 AM. Don't know why they got up so late but anyway they did. Maybe the day won't be so long now.

Suppose you are in the corn field already. Boy wish I was there too. Can hardly wait until I get in the corn field because I would like to do quite a bit of it and I also have to pick corn so that I will have some money to come up there. I have sent for part of your Christmas present. But now don't ask what it is because I don't want to tell you. ha Well they came in from the chores now and my news is just simply all. Did you show your folks that sample of the dress goods? And what did they say about it? If you didn't, it is all right, you don't have to if you don't want to. I just wondered about it. So just do as you want to.

Dad just now tried to make me give it up to come up there. Said if I want to buy a couple of sows I have to stay at home, but I just told him that I don't have them yet and I am coming up there if nothing keeps me from it.

Well Sweetheart my news is just plum all so will close for des mol *[this time]*. Will be looking for a big fat letter from you. Wishing you God's richest blessings. Good luck to you till we meet again. Love and best wishes.

From a true loving sweetheart,
Susie Ann Miller

A few days later Amos got out his writing tablet. How would he ever make it without Susie's letters to keep him going? He wondered if his letters meant as much to her. What would it be like spending every day of his life with her? He couldn't wait to find out but for now he would live on the letters of love.

Nov. 24, 1957

Dearest loved Sweetheart,

Greetings of my purest love to you. I received your ever-ever so welcome letter yesterday. Boy was I glad to have such a big letter from you.

I tell you sweetheart I sure was disappointed Friday when I didn't get a letter from you. I can't tell you Sweetheart how I felt the rest of the day and also Saturday until I got your letter. I sure wondered what happened that there wasn't a letter on Friday from you.

Wonder how you are in the line of health? For me I am feeling fine except a little love sick for you Sweetheart. But guess I'll make it if you come up at Christmas time, which I am really glad you will you know. It sure seems pretty far off yet until Christmas. But it will be only three Sundays without today before we will be seeing each other again. But I sure wish you were here today. Guess I'll have the day by myself again. My folks and the little boys were invited over to Levi Yoders place. But I don't know where I want to go, so guess I will just stay at home all day. So why don't you come up to me Sweetheart? Guess I might as well forget about it, because I can't come down there today. But hope next time I do come down there it will be to stay for good.

You know Sweetheart I sure am looking forward to the time that we can be together forever and have a happy life together. You know Sweetheart that that's quite a ways off yet but hope nothing happens until then, so that we can still get married like we planned. Yes I told my folks that you are planning to be up here over Christmas. Yes Sweetheart I think I am just as glad as you are that they didn't care about us getting married then. You know Sweetheart that's one thing I sure hope for when the time comes when we get married. But guess I'll be just as glad when the wedding is over with, so that we are on our own then. Don't you think so Sweetheart? I got my cousin's letter written, I wrote it before I finished your letter.

I was sure glad to hear that you are coming another route than what I did. I won't have to worry so much now if you come on the train. But don't worry that I won't be there to meet you when you get here. Yes, that's all right with me if you write a letter on Wednesday that way I won't have to wait as long for a letter from you.

I guess you are right, maybe if you got the flu from somebody else you wouldn't get over it so quick. I didn't think bad about you that you didn't take that job for $21a week. Was glad that you thought about getting your letters and that you don't like to work in such places unless you have to. I sure would have come and ate supper if I only would have been down there, you know that I would have, now don't you? ha

Well, I am just doing whatever happens, just a little of everything. Got the cobs all out of the corn crib now. But I still haven't got the cribs ready for corn. Sure wish I would have the cribs done and would be picking corn, hard and heavy. No I don't have that toolshed roof done yet. Don't know when I will get it done if this weather keeps up. Oh there's a white roof on it, but it's just snow. ha

Yes, I guess you are right, you probably wouldn't think about my beard. We probably would have had too many other things to talk about if only you were here to talk about them. I would feel a lot happier that way.

I knew they didn't have to leave their beards grow until they are published to be married, and I sure like it about that part too. Now don't think you are dumb and silly and all that stuff because you aren't Sweetheart. If I thought you were that way I wouldn't be loving you the way I do. And you know that I don't think you are that way. I was just hoping you didn't think I was silly and dumb for the way I do things sometimes.

Yes, that was Junior Swartz who had a little boy. I guess his sister Carolyn was pretty sick the other week. They were eating dinner when all of a sudden she let herself fall over on Anna's lap. They said she turned white and blue around her lips, and she was unconscious for two hours. I guess they told all the children to come home, they thought she would pass away any minute. They said her brothers fainted when they saw her, guess it was such a shock to them. They called the doctor, but said he wasn't there very long until she came to. The doctor said he didn't know what else it could have been unless it was like the hard flu they had back in 1918. They said there was a man in Oelwein that had the same thing, and he died right away. But guess Carolyn is okay again - - the last I heard.

I wasn't tired of reading your long and lovely letter either. I was just glad to get such a nice big fat letter from you. I should go and do the dinner chores as it's 12:30 PM already. So long.

Here I am again. I just got back from the creek. I went down to see if the ice was still okay. Johnny and Joni have been skating on it for the last two days or so. Guess I will try it out after dinner, it's 1:00 PM already. I am not very hungry now even if it's late. We didn't get up very early this morning, it was 9:00 AM when we were eating breakfast. So now you can see how lazy we are. ha I can hardly wait until I hit that ice this afternoon.

Boy, I can tell you ice skating is really a lot of fun. Anyway if you know how and don't fall down all the time. Of course I am no expert. ha But I can skate just as fast backwards as Johnny and Joni can skate forwards. You know, it comes in handy – you can skate backwards when there is a big crowd and you are playing tag or hockey. Sure wish you were here to go along with me and watch me skate. Of course you wouldn't see very much if you would see me. But it would be more fun if you were here anyway. Don't you think so? Of course it isn't a very big space, but guess it's big enough to try it out. But it would be more fun on a big river where you can skate for about three miles. Last winter Crazy Mel and Menno Mullet and I skated two miles in twelve minutes. But I tell you we were glad to stay when we got there. Well, maybe I better stop bragging about our skating. ha

What are you doing today? As for me I haven't done very much yet so far. Don't know what I'll do to bring the afternoon around, guess skate a little more. Don't think I could sleep if I wanted to, went to bed the last three evenings at eight o'clock. So why don't you come and bother me, so I can lose some sleep again, how about it?

You know, Sweetheart, the night my folks left here, we got a carload of company from Ohio. I didn't recognize them at first even though we went to the same school they did when they were living here. I bet you wonder who they were? Well, it was Susan Troyer and her husband. They also had her brother Henry Jr., Sister Alma, Elizabeth, and Anna along with them. Boy, they sure looked a lot different than when they lived here. Guess it was their car as Elizabeth was driving when they drove in here. I think they are members of a Mennonite church.

I got a bigger letter written already than I thought that I would. Don't know if I'll get it as big as your letter was or not. Hope so, that way you can read for a while. Maybe until you are done reading you will be tired of all my junk that I usually write. Don't you think so? Boy sure seems like I can make a lot of mistakes when I am writing with ink. Now don't tell me I don't. Well, Sweetie, maybe I better go and eat dinner and try to skate before it melts enough that water comes on the top. It was nice and smooth when I was down there about a half an hour ago. Can't think of very much worthwhile writing right now anyway, so guess I'll go and eat.

Here I am again. Just got back from skating. Sure is warm in here, guess I got warmed up when I was skating. You know, the days weren't so long as I was afraid they would be, while my folks were gone. Guess it helped because Johnny and Joni weren't in school all week because their teacher was sick. You know I heard something about you, didn't know what to think about it. ha ha Heard you had to go with my dad and your dad on the wagon to go out to Ezras. Was kind of wondering why you had to ride on the wagon instead of Sadie. Or did you want to? It would have been nicer for a nice girl like you to ride in the buggy. Wouldn't it? At least I think so. Of course you probably think I am kind of kindish to think so or to ask about it. But I was just kind of nosy I guess. Just so you don't feel bad about me for the way I wrote.

You know, Sweetheart, it sure is lonesome here today. All alone and nothing to do but to write you a letter. I sure wish you were here today. Talking would always go better than writing. Say, while I think about it, I want to ask you a question and I want you to answer it. When you come up here for Christmas and our Sale, were you going to stay then until we move or not? Sure hope you are.

You know, I can hardly wait until the sale is past and everything is settled for so that we are ready to move. I am so done with this Iowa that I don't know what to do with myself, or I mean Buck County. You know, it just isn't fun here without you. Seems like I don't enjoy myself like I used to before I knew we were moving to Mo. Guess if I wouldn't care what I do here I would have more fun. But since I have you I want to act like I should. You probably wouldn't think much about me if I would tear around with those rough boys, would you? Anyway I can tell you I sure feel a lot different since I have you then I did before. Before I had you it just seemed like I didn't care what I did.

You know it sure makes me feel good to think of us going on our own in about a year. Just seems too good to be true, but I sure hope it will come true some day. But seems like I can hardly wait for that day to come. Just think, when we move we won't have to be writing letters all the time either. Then we can see each other every Sunday and maybe sometimes through the week.

You don't know how good it makes me feel to know somebody loves me and cares for me. You know, Sweetheart, it makes a guy feel more like doing something when he knows he can depend on somebody to marry someday.

Maybe I am silly to write this but it's just the way I feel about you. I never felt so good in my life to think of having you for my wife someday. I just can't write in words how much I love you and the way that you are. Guess I might as well write something else. It just makes me wish more that you were here so that I could talk to you and tell you how I feel about you.

But guess I might as well forget it until Christmas then we can do our talking if nothing happens until then. I hope that nothing happens so that you can't come. Well you know what? I got your Christmas present already but didn't get what I was going to get you at first, but it's something as good and even better then what I was going to get. It's something we can use together after we are married. Well I probably wrote enough to make you wonder what it is. But don't go asking me because I don't want to tell you yet. Mom and Dad both thought it was pretty nice. Didn't know what else I could've got for you that you would've liked better. So hope you like what I did get you. Well maybe I better read this letter to see if I wrote everything that I was going to. Maybe I wrote too much already.

Tomorrow one of the local boys will have a trial in Chicago for not going to serve his 1-W service when he was called to. They could have saved a lot of expense if he would have gone to 1-W service. Guess he thinks he's too good to go do something like that. Maybe I shouldn't write this way, but it's just the way I feel about it. If he would have gone to 1-W service, his wife could've gone with him and he could've worn his Amish clothing to do his service. But I am afraid this way, it will turn out just like it did for another guy. That guy was sentenced to jail for two months and a fine to pay of $5000 which of course he couldn't pay. Now he has to serve his term in jail, and he could have served in 1-W if he would have wanted to.

If it goes that same way for this guy tomorrow at this trial, he will get his hair cut and English clothes and be without his wife. Seems to me, I would lots rather work for 1-W service and take my wife along with me, instead of the way he is doing. Don't you think so? Just write me and let me know what you think about it. I told you what I think about it.

I don't know if I wrote you or not that [name omitted] came back again and is planning to start up a harness shop. The way they say, he bought some land off of Willie's farm, and they are putting up a building already. But I just sometimes wonder how long he will keep that up. For the ways he acted other times when he came home. Was just hoping he would keep it up. But a guy can never tell, the way he has acted so many times already. He even tried to get a divorce the last time he went away. I guess he would have got one too if his parents and his wife wouldn't have done something about it.

But you don't have to worry about me leaving you like he did his wife. Of course you aren't my wife, but I still hope you are someday. When you are my wife you won't have to worry about me leaving you. Because I am never <u>never</u> going to do something like that. Unless something happens to my health that I don't know what I am doing. But I hope nothing will ever happen. Well maybe I wrote enough of this stuff already. Maybe I better write something else.

I got one more sheet written now than you did in your letter. But maybe I better keep writing so that I will get enough written to make up for your sixteen sides that you wrote. Even if I have more they probably won't mean as much as your sixteen did to me. But maybe if I keep writing I'll get a bigger letter from you next time. But maybe I better not make it too big or I won't get it all in one envelope. Don't you think so? Well just seems like I can't think of much more to write, so maybe I better stop until Monday morning. It's 4:30 PM already, guess time went a little faster then I thought it did. Guess it went faster because I was writing you a letter all this time.

Here I am again, didn't go very far, started to read your letter again then I found a question that I didn't answer for you. NO, I didn't show that dress sample to my folks yet. I just thought there would be plenty time enough later on. So I just didn't take time to show them. Maybe we can show it when you come up here for Christmas. And don't you let them talk you into giving it up to come up here, because I want you to come. I got to have somebody with me to pass the time.

Well, maybe I better quit now until Monday morning or I may have so many sheets that it will take you half a day to read them.

Hi, here I am again, just got home from the Singing and it's twelve o'clock. Would have plenty of time to have a date yet tonight if only you were here. My arms are oh so empty and it's so lonely here without you. Sure wish you were here tonight. It just seems like I should see you here, but I don't . Well I guess I might as well forget it for tonight, because it can't be helped. Anyway the Singing was just at Abe Yoder's tonight. But sure wasn't a very big Singing. I don't think half of them were there. But we still had kind of fun. But you don't need to think of one minute that I didn't think of you because I was thinking of you all the time.

Well, you know this is the biggest letter I ever wrote to you. But don't know if it will mean much to you. But no matter how much it means to you. I am still looking for a big fat lovely letter from you.

You know I didn't think I could ever write so much. But guess I just wrote whatever that came to my mind. So if you don't want to read all of it, you don't have to. Good time to tell you when I am almost done isn't it?

Anyway I hope you won't get tired of reading all my nonsense that I wrote. Well, I am getting kind of sleepy so guess I'll go to bed. But I sure wouldn't if you were here. So goodnight, I'll see you in my dreams.

Good morning, how are you feeling this morning? For me I am just feeling fine. Guess I am feeling a little too good, didn't loose enough sleep last night. I had a little mishap this morning. Well it's a little after seven and I'm waiting on breakfast to get ready so thought I'd write a couple lines before breakfast.

Well, about that little mishap this morning. Hope you don't think I am kindish after you read it. The way it was, Johnny was teasing our dog, Shep, with an ear of corn. He just held it up high enough so that Shep couldn't reach it. So I went and took a hold of his hand and told Shep to get it. Then I happen to pinch Johnny a little so of course he came after me. Guess I better go, they are calling me for breakfast. Here I am again, I ran back to the hay pile with Johnny after me. Of course I had a hay fork in my hand because I was giving the horses hay. I had the tine turned up, then I happen to kick against the fork myself and it punched into my lip. But isn't very bad because it doesn't hurt anymore. Guess that's what can happen when a person is silly horsing around. Don't you think so?

But it isn't so bad that I couldn't give you a big hug if you were only here so I could give you one. Well I better finish this letter, I need to ride down to Willie Yoder's to find out for sure if there is going to be school today. See you later.

Here I am again. I was waiting on the boys to go downstairs so I could finish your letter. Well anyway I didn't even go down to Willie's. When I got outside there was smoke coming from the chimney on the schoolhouse, so I knew they were having school. Well seems like I can't think of anything to write anymore, you blame me? You probably think I should have stopped long before this. Anyway this is I bet the biggest letter you ever got. But maybe it isn't the best one. Might start picking corn tomorrow if I get the cribs ready today. So long Sweetheart, wishing you God's richest blessing.

From a true loving Sweetheart,
Amos Miller

The letter ended up being so big that Susie had to pay additional postage on it. But that was okay--Susie didn't mind. She'd pay additional postage any day as long as Amos wrote those big fat letters. Susie kept up her love letters to her future husband.

Chapter 22

# The Courtship Letters Continue

Nov. 26, 1957

Dearest loved Sweetheart,

Greetings of love. Wonder how this finds you in the line of health? I am just as usual. Sure am a little disappointed though because I am not picking corn yet. Thought sure I would be starting today. Now I'll have to wait until tomorrow that will leave only three days for this week because I will not pick any on Thanksgiving. Don't have to much time to pick corn but guess I'll have enough to take me to Iowa and home again and still have some left for other things.

I don't have your letter yet because it is only 9:30 AM at least I hope I'll get a letter today. Don't know will the mailman be gone when we get out there or not. But hope so and he better leave a letter there for me from you. Guess I'll go to church in PM. Emanuel Mullet from Buchanan Co, Iowa is here. So there is church in PM. I suppose you probably know him. Anyway I do if you don't. ha

Oh yes, your mother told me that you have bought my Christmas present already. She didn't say what it is though. Gel? You knew what to get if I didn't tell you. Anything is all right so long as it comes from you.

What are you'alls shoffing*[up to/working at]*? Me? Well I am writing just now as you can see. Yesterday I was out to Ezra's to do their washing. This morning I sewed on my new gray dress. Don't have it finished, but am waiting on gray thread. Haven't got too much left to do. I hope to be picking corn by this time tomorrow morning.

You know it is just three more weeks and we will be seeing each other again. But these five weeks aren't near as long as those first four weeks were. Oh I just thought those weeks were the longest weeks I have ever had. I don't know what makes these weeks so short. I guess because I am also planning on going up there again. Of course I have enough to do yet before I come up there guess that is another reason they go so fast. Because I am busy all the time. Haven't got much time to sit around and think about this and that.

You know I didn't get any money from Ezra's last week, but they said they would give me $6 this week. So maybe I can do a little something for myself. I have to get me some hens to pick corn and it doesn't take just a little bit of money for that. I also have to send for your Christmas present yet. Well it seems I can't think of anything more to write just now so I will go do something else. Maybe I will know more tonight. So here I go.

Hi - - this is now schund evening. It is 6:30 PM and we got home from Church about an hour ago.

I received your very welcome letter this morning just a little before dinner. Mom and Dad were to Jamesport this morning so they went into the post office and got the mail. You know what? They had to pay $.03 more for the letter but anyway I really enjoyed it. It was worth the $.03 more. But I have to do pretty good if I want to beat you in writing. Because I just know I can't write that much.

I talked with Lydia Schrock Sunday evening but I don't know more than I did. But I expect I'll have to go by myself. Maybe I won't have to all the way. I have been thinking about writing a girl in Johnson Co, Iowa to go with me from there. I don't know will it do me any good or not, but at least I can try it. I'll wait though until after Thursday. Lydia said she would let me know by Thursday. So if she doesn't go with me I'll try the other girl in Iowa.

Oh yes, I wish you were here for Thursday evening. Guess we will have a taffy pulling here Thursday evening. Really wish you were here to help me pull. I'll just sit back and let the others do the pulling. I will probably be busy putting in flavor and cutting it into eating size. Guess I'll get someone to help me make some to bring along up there when I come. So long, supper is ready.

Well supper is past but dishes aren't washed yet. Sadie has to wash them. I may dry them if I get that far. Guess I'll read your letter and answer your questions. Maybe by that time I'll have enough written. ha

Boy you know I sure would have been there Sunday if I could have been, but I guess I'll have to wait a couple more weeks. In three weeks at this time I hope I'll be where you are.

Yes about that marrying business, I too hope we can do as we planned. But your mother didn't talk too favorable about it when they were here. I talked with her and she told me what she said, but I believe when the time comes they will say yes without any hesitation.

Because they would have let Ezra's get married about a year sooner then they did if my folks would have done it. Anyway I don't think we have to worry that they won't let us. Do you think we will? It is quite a ways off yet, but after you are here and we see each other every Sunday evening the time will be near before we realize it. gel? Anyway I believe it will be that way. Yes, I think we will both be glad and happy when the time comes and when it is over with.

Yes, if you see your letter coming back you know I couldn't read it. ha But don't worry I'll get it made. It isn't hard to read. Now you know that I don't think you are silly and dumb because if I did I probably wouldn't write to you.

Yes I had heard about Carolyn Swartz being so sick. I guess that flu is pretty tough.

Why wouldn't I see much? I think I'd see quite a lot if I saw you skating. Maybe I'll see you skating when I come up there. ha I bet you went two miles in twelve minutes. But I didn't smell anything and I don't think I would if you bragged ever so much. ha I was in church Sunday at Chrissie Ropp's. I stayed for supper and Singing. I walked home after the Singing. It wasn't too warm to be walking but we didn't freeze. ha We won't have to worry about walking when you get here.

Well I know I won't get such a big letter written that you did but hope it will be okay. It just seems my thinker doesn't work very good tonight for some reason. You don't write any junk anyway. It is all news to me.

Did you have some good skating? Hope so anyway. We wouldn't dare go on the ice here yet. Of course the coldest we have had here was 12 degrees. Cold enough but not so very cold, gel net*[don't you think so]*?

It would have been nicer to ride in the buggy but I said I would go on the wagon. I didn't care too much. Nope, I don't think you were kindish to ask about it because I would have asked about you too.

Talking goes better then writing any day but guess writing will have to do if we can't talk.

Well I don't know yet what will I say until you come or not. Guess we will just have to wait and see what I decide when the time comes.

Yes I am glad to hear you want to act like you should. Hope you will enjoy yourself when you move down here. I am afraid I wouldn't think very much of you if you were with those rough boys.

Yes, it sure makes me feel good to know someone loves me and cares for me. It gives me a better feeling to go on and work.

Yes, we may just as well save some writing and then talk when we see each other at Christmas. Yes, you did make me gwunnerich about what you got me for Christmas, but I guess I can wait until Christmas to see it.

Sure wonder how Dan's Abie came out with his trial. I feel about it just like you do. I really think he should have gone to do some 1-W work. He would have it lots nicer anyway. Is Joni Petersheim still in jail?

Yes, I knew [name omitted] was back. Sure hope he does stick to it.

Your letter means just as much to me as mine did to you. I don't know anyway what I would do if I didn't get these letters from you.

Well, maybe I shouldn't have told your mother what I did. I told her that I sent for some dress goods and told her also that I sent you a sample. But you can wait to show it until I come up there. If you haven't showed it yet.

I sure thought about you Sunday night when I got home from the Singing but couldn't do more than go to bed. You know I don't think you were kindish as to what you did to Johnny because I feel like teasing too sometimes. Guess you know that already.

Yes, this was the biggest and the best letter I ever got. I sure was pleased with it anyway. Can't think of anything more to write so guess I'll go to bed and finish in the morning. Good night, Sweetheart, see you in my dreams.

Good morning, how are you this morning? I am just as usual and hope you are the same. Would be sorry to hear different.

I wonder what you will do today? I guess I'll have my first day picking corn today. I wanted to begin last week already. I can hardly stand it that I haven't picked any yet. I don't know for sure but I think maybe I'll get $.15 a bushel. It isn't too much if I have to scoop which I have to until Dad comes and helps pick corn over there too.

It is clear this morning and not so very cold so guess it won't be too bad. Well sheet is full and news is all so must hike on.

With Luck, Love, and Best Wishes,

From a true Loving Sweetheart

Well, here I am again. Guess I won't go corn picking today after all. I suppose you wonder why, gel? Well I just couldn't get anybody to go with me today. There is a quilting at Dan Stutzman's and Sadie is bound to go to the quilting. Levi has to go to school and of course Dad won't do it to go, so long as he isn't finished at home. I guess I'll have to give it up till Friday being tomorrow is Thanksgiving. I don't know what makes them feel so much better to want to do just opposite from me, but maybe some day it won't be like that.

I just dressed a turkey for tomorrow. I wish you were here to help eat it. We have to go out to Ezra's with it, sure wish you were here to go along.

I hope by next week I will have enough money to send for your Christmas present. I don't want to wait until too near Christmas because it may not even be here by Christmas.

Oh yes, this morning the milkman came through that little road that goes east from us. When he got almost here at that mud hole he got stuck. Boy he really acted around there for about half an hour trying to get out by himself. He finally wondered if Dad has horses harnessed. Dad said he can't pull him out with the horses so he went to our neighbor. He finally got out after an hour being stuck in the mud hole. But you should just see the mud hole that is there now.

Well, guess I better go get ready to go to the quilting. Don't know anything worth writing anymore anyway. God be with you till we meet again.

With lots of love from a true Loving Sweetheart,

Susie Ann Miller

Amos's response to Susie's letter of Nov 26, 1957.

Nov. 29, 1957

Dearest Loved Sweetheart,

Wonder how this finds you in the line of health? For me I am just like usual. But a lot happier since I got your ever so welcome letter today. You know I could hardly wait until the mailman went today. I could hardly wait so I could read your letter which I was expecting from you.

Wonder if you got started to pick corn today now. I know just how you feel planning to get started and then not even start.

Don't worry for someday it will work right for you anyway if I am with you. I don't think I'll want anything opposite from what you want to do like they did for you. Don't you think so? You know it's 7:30 PM and I haven't had supper yet. I feel like I could use some. I guess Mom is baking apple shortcake. That's why it's taking so long. I probably would have had a nice big supper already if you would have made it. Don't you think so?

I wonder how the weather is down there? This afternoon it sure turned cold. It got eight degrees colder from the time I went in for dinner until I went out again. I guess it was 8/0 when the boys came home from school tonight. But it's warmed up since to 16/0. Must go for supper.

Here I am again. I had supper and it's 8 PM. Johnny and Joni are washing dishes and you can see what I am doing. Did you get started to pick corn today and how much did you pick? Now don't be ashamed to tell me how much you picked because you probably picked all that was good for you. If you do scoop corn, take it easy so that you don't harm yourself. I would be sorry if you did any harm.

I picked some corn today too. I went out in the field at 7 AM and picked enough corn to grind feed for the cows which was about ten bushel. When I got done grinding I greased the wagon and done other odds and ends. I was wishing the mailman would come so that I could read your letter and feel like doing something. My wish came true, the mailman just went.

We had a late dinner so I didn't get out to pick more corn till 2 PM. By that time it was pretty cold. So I worked pretty fast all afternoon to keep myself warm. I husked sixteen rows this afternoon, but that was just in the small field west of the barn. Now I don't want you to think that I am bragging again. From 2 PM to 5:30 PM I husked 60 bushels. I didn't think I husked that much but it figured out that way.

You probably husked that much all day today didn't you? With what I picked in AM and PM I had a total of 70 bushels today. I was hoping if I picked all day and got early starts that I could pick 60 bushel in AM and PM with a total of 120 bushel a day. But don't know if I will be that good or not. Do you think I will?

You know, I am feeling a little tired tonight for some reason. I wonder why? I have kind of a cold sticking in my nose tonight. I wish you were here. Maybe it would leave me then. Well, maybe I better re-read your letter and answer your questions so that I know something to write. Have to go now. They want to get ready for bed.

I am back again and it's 9 PM already. I don't know how much I'll get written tonight. I feel kind of sleepy already. Your folks probably thought that I am kind of silly that I wrote you such a big letter that they had to pay $.03 more to get it. What did they say about it anyway? Now come on -- tell me just what they said.

You know I didn't expect to get as big a letter from you as the one I wrote you, but yours meant just as much to me as if you would have written as a big a letter as I did.

You said you talked to my mother about us getting married, but you didn't write what she said about it. What did she say? You wrote she didn't talk to favorable, so I wondered what she did say. I don't think we have to worry that they won't say yes when the time comes. No, you won't have to worry about walking home from the Singing when I get down there. You know you won't have to, don't you?

Boy, if I would have known that you had to walk home from the Singing last Sunday night, I couldn't have rested very easy, but I guess there wouldn't have been anything that I could have done about it.

Yes, I had good skating. I wished you would have been here. It would have been lots more fun that way. Don't you think so? Yes, it was in the paper today that Dan's Abie is sentenced to jail for one year. Joni Petershiem is still in jail serving his time.

I don't feel like you shouldn't have told my mother that you sent for those dress goods. I don't think she thought bad about it that you did.

I wish I could get some corn picking for $.15 per bushel. I wouldn't hesitate very long if I could get a job like that.

Well, it's 9:30 PM and I am not in bed, but I guess I'll go as I am sleepy. I'll see you in my dreams. Good night.

Good morning, how are you feeling? I am feeling a little better this morning than I did last night. Well, Sweetie, you're probably in the field picking corn already this morning. I should be but I am not and it's 7:30 AM already.

We had kind of cold weather this morning. It was zero degrees. Do you think that's cold enough?

Yes, I sure wish I was there on Thanksgiving night to help you pull taffy. You probably would have enjoyed yourself better don't you think so?

You know, Mother just now told me that I could wait until Monday to send this letter. She said I should hurry and get to work, but I told her that I want to send your letter today. I knew you would be disappointed if you didn't get a letter next Monday. You know, I should hurry but I am afraid I'll forget some things I was going to write.

I have nine rows to pick yet in the small field west of the barn. They want me to hurry and finish this field so I can get started on the popcorn field which is about two miles north of here.

I don't know what ails me lately. It seems like I awake every night dreaming and ever time I think of you. I guess because I have so much work to do it wakes me up during the night thinking about it.

I am going to try and be done picking corn by Christmas, but I am afraid I won't make it unless we make a frolic. But I'm sure going to try and be done by Christmas, because I want to be done when you get here.

I thought of a lot of things I wanted to write, but I am too much in a hurry to remember them. Now don't go spending all your money just to get a guy like me a Christmas present. Because I don't need anything that costs much and you know I don't. If you get something that cost so much I might have to be ashamed of myself if I didn't spend as much as you did.

Seems like I am thinking of you all the time even when I am husking corn. Seems like there's nothing else so good to think about. Seems like I am day dreaming all the time when I am husking corn, and it's about you. I usually think of us being together and how nice I would treat you, also how much nicer it would be if we were together I don't know what else all I think, probably couldn't write it all down. Just seems like I can't think of what I was going to write. But hope you are satisfied with what I did write. I hope to do better next time. This letter is only half as big as the other letter was, but hope it means just as much to you. God be with you till we meet again. Love, Luck, and Best Wishes.

With Lots of Love, a true Loving Sweetheart,

Amos Miller

Susie's response to Amos's November 29th letter.

Dec. 2, 1957

Dearest Loved Sweetheart,

Greetings of my best love to you. How does this find you in the line of health? For me I am just as usual except a little sleepy. ha

I suppose you wonder why I am sleepy, gel? Well, it was 12:30 AM already when Sadie and I came home last night from the Singing.

I didn't get very far with my letter writing until I left it again. Dad said he would give anybody $.50 if they would feed the pigs for him, so I went to feed them and now I have half a dollar. Pretty easy made money, isn't it?

But now to go on with my story about last night. Sadie and I were there with our rig and Eli Bontrager's girls were there with their rig, so we decided after the Singing we would strike out together and do some cutting up. Boy, we sure had a time. ha Singing was at Joe Hochstetlers. Our first stop was at Amos Mast's. We didn't do very much there because they had the doors all locked. William Hochstetler was there with Sarah. The second stop was at Simon Hostetler's. We had the most fun there. It was Abie Ropp and Susie Bontrager. The third stop was Chrissie Ropp's. Amos Mast was there. They had their things all hid, so we didn't have very much to do there. The fourth and last stop was at Dan Stutzman's. Phineas and Benjamin Schrock were there. Well, guess that wasn't the last stop though because we went home from there. ha

Supper is now past. Sadie is washing the dishes. It is 7:00 PM, so I will have some time left to finish this tonight. I hope, if I don't get too sleepy.

What did you do yesterday? Probably go to church. huh? Well, I was in church, it wasn't our church but went because Abe Bontrager was there.

You know, Ezra's gave me $6 last week and they are going to give me the rest yet before I leave for Iowa. I was hoping I could pick enough corn to pay my way to Iowa and back again. Of course, I can't but every little bit helps.

Oh yes, I have some good news for you. Well, maybe you wouldn't say it is good news but I hope you will. At least it would be good news for me if it came from you. But maybe I better tell you or you may get mad at me. ha What would I do if you got mad at me? Boy, I don't hope that ever, ever happens.

Well, anyway here comes the news, whether it is good or bad. ha.

Guess I'll leave Missouri, Thursday evening the 12th. I will be in Hazleton Friday PM at 4:00 and hoping to see you there. Verna Bontrager wants to go to Johnson Co., Iowa and doesn't want to go by herself, so I decided I would just go a little sooner than I had planned. So just think of it, Sweetheart, just a little over a week and we will be seeing each other if nothing happens. I suppose the time will be here before I am ready. Because I have enough to do yet.

Pick corn this week and then I would have only a few days left to get all my things ready. I have some sewing I want to do yet. But if I have a lot of work to do, the time won't be so long for me until then. You see if I go with Verna, I won't have to go by myself all the way. Of course, I don't know for sure but I may not have to go by myself all the way. I wrote a girl in Johnson about going along. I haven't heard from her yet but expect an answer Wednesday. I hope she will go along.

Well, guess I'll read your very welcome letter which I received today. Maybe I'll know more to write then. Yes, I started picking corn last Friday. But such a day as it ended up to. Well, the end wasn't as bad as the middle. ha. We got an awful late start Friday morning. It was 9:30 already when we got in the field. When we were in the field it started raining and then turned to snow. Boy was the stuff ever wet and was it ever cold. Guess I didn't even get ten bushels out. But hope it will go better tomorrow.

I know everything will go all right when we get to living together.

Well, now supper may have been ready if I had made it. But just how big it would have been I can't tell. ha

We are having pretty fair weather here. It isn't so awful cold. Of course it isn't just exactly warm either. ha I would have gone with you to eat supper if I could have, but hope I can before long.

You don't have to think that I would think that you would be bragging. I want you to feel free to write or tell me anything you want to. But anyway I think you did pretty good to pick 60 bushels in three hours and a half. I feel pretty proud of you, Sweetheart.

I think you will be good enough to pick 120 bushels corn in a day. I suppose you wouldn't have any cold if I was there. But I have a little cold tonight, so I guess we are even now. ha

They didn't say very much about the big letter. Mother just teased me and said she wants to see my catalogue too. She said maybe she wants to send for something. ha But anyway don't feel bad about it because she was just teasing. You know, they have really changed since you were here. I guess they like what they saw and liked your ways too.

Your mother didn't say much about us getting married next fall. She just said she told you that you would be pretty young. So Dan's Abie is now aw*[also]* in jail. How long does Joni Petersheim still have to be in jail? Wonder what Abie Martha will do now? How pitiful it is. They are married and he is now in jail. They will probably enjoy their married life now, I think it is a shame. . .

I sure would hate to have it much colder than zero. Booooo it makes me shiver just to think about it.

If you would make a frolic to pick corn you wouldn't have to work as hard. That way you would get done before Christmas.

This last letter meant just as much to me as any of the others did. And you don't have to worry about being ashamed because I am not spending such an awful lot of money. Not as much as I should but hope it will do.

Well, I am just plain rattled out for tonight and it is bedtime for me. Little sleepy head. ha Maybe I'll know more in the morning. So good night, I'll be seeing you in my dreams because I usually do.

Oh, yes, I made some fudge tonight. I wish you were here to help eat it. So long Sweet Dreams.

Good morning, how are you this morning? I am feeling fine and dandy. I guess I'll go corn picking this morning. The man just came to get us. So I don't know how much I'll get done. I have to quit and go because he doesn't want to wait long.

Love, Luck, and Best Wishes from a true

Loving Sweetheart, Susie Ann Miller

Amos's response to Susie's letter of December 2nd.

Dec. 5, 1957

Dearest Loved Sweetheart,

Greetings of my Best Love to you. I wonder how this finds you in the boat of health? For me I am feeling just fine and a lot happier since I received your ever so welcome letter today.

Boy was I ever glad for that lovely letter. It wasn't so awful big, but it sure meant a lot to me. Well, it's 7 PM and I just started to write your letter. We didn't have supper yet as Dad is still working in the shop. Seems like everybody is bringing things to get fixed just because we want to get some corn picked. Dad was going to help me husk corn, but seems like he can't get out of the shop.

Was I ever overjoyed to hear that you are coming a week from Friday instead of waiting longer. You know, I was so overjoyed I felt like jumping up and down. Boy, you know this way I will have only next Sunday by myself. Then after that you will be here and boy am I glad. I sure thought a lot about you these last days, wishing that you would come sooner. So guess my wishing came true.

I can hardly wait until Friday in a week, but guess the time will be here before I know it. I have so much work to do yet, am still not done husking corn. I am not even half way done yet. You probably think I am kind of slow at it, but seems like everything wants to go backwards for me these past days. But maybe it will go better when you are up here to comfort me.

You know I didn't even husk corn today, because I hurt too much. Last night when I quit, my left arm and wrist were so sore that I couldn't even move them without hurting real bad. I couldn't even put the horses away, so I had Dad put them away. All I could do was walk around and hold my wrist. I guess I must have strained it pretty hard when I was husking. Even when I held it, my wrist hurt every time my heart beat, so I went and soaked it in warm vinegar water.

Then while I was soaking my wrist, Emanuel came and told us to come up to Alvin's for ice cream. They had brought a freezer full of ice cream over to Alvin's for a surprise on Katie as it was her birthday. So then we went up there. At 10:30 PM I told Dad to give me the keys to the house that I am going home, that they can come when they are ready. Joni and I went home, Johnny was sleeping so we left him sit there. So you probably know how I feel tonight, not very sleepy. ha

Anyway, don't go worrying about my wrist, tonight it feels better. Don't know if I will husk corn right away in the morning or not. At noon I put a warm cloth and Ben-gay on my arm and it helped a lot. I might try to husk some corn in the afternoon.

Well, you know, I finally got that elevator of ours working, so in the morning I want to unload the corn I husked yesterday to see if it really does work. ha Willie Yoder was kind of nice to us. He said we could use his new motor to run the elevator as he isn't using it right now anyway. He had bought his new motor awhile back and hadn't even used it yet. He said we might as well use it so we don't have to take our motor out of the shop. So long, supper is ready.

Here I am again. Supper is over so here I am writing again. I guess I'll re-read your letter so I know what questions I need to answer. Yes, last Sunday I went to church and was almost late, but of course I wouldn't have been late if I were down there.

You know I wouldn't get mad at you, no matter what you would do. I can't see how I could ever get mad at you for so nice a girl that you are, gel net? You know it would be good news to me to hear that you were coming sooner gel you did? Well, anyway it sure was good news to me. I sure feel good to know that next Sunday will be the last Sunday that I will have to go to the Singing by myself before you come.

You just don't know how much happier I am since I know you are coming sooner. You don't have to worry that I won't be there to meet you, unless something really bad would happen that I couldn't come. But am sure Mother would meet you if I couldn't.

I hope nothing comes in the way that would keep me from meeting you. I will probably take my horse and the folks top buggy to come and get you, that way not everybody can see us anyway, if that's okay with you?

I sure hope that girl from Johnson can come with you up here, and I sure am glad you don't have to come by yourself all the way, all alone. Just wish I was there to come with you.

Well anyway if I do come down there again, I hope it will be to stay for good. Then we can be more together then we are now. I was sorry to hear you had such a bad day to start husking corn, hope your future days will be nicer. I sure hope you can go with me to supper before long which is only a week off yet.

I just can't tell you how glad I am that you are coming sooner then you were going too. I guess I better go they want to make ready for bed.

Here I am again, I'll try to finish answering your questions tonight because I might not have time in the morning, am a little sleepy already.

It made me feel good to know you thought I did pretty good husking 60 bushel in three and a half hours. It also made me feel good to know I can tell you anything that I want too. You know, I sure am glad you are the way you are. You are so understanding and don't make fun of me for things that I tell you. Others have made fun of me already for the way I say things sometimes.

You know talking sure would go better than writing which I hope to do when we meet Friday. I just might talk so much to you that you will get a head ache from listening to me.

I haven't heard how long Joni Petersheim has to serve in jail yet. I guess Abie Martha is going down to Missouri where they are starting a new settlement.

Now don't you worry that I can't read your scribbling, your scribbling is nicer than my good writing.

Well, here I am on sheet 11 already. I didn't think I'd write this much when I started. I don't want to write more than this sheet full or we might not know anything to say when you get up here, if I write it all now. I am afraid I couldn't write it all that we are going to say, you think so? I am not worried that I won't have anything to say when you get here. I am getting sleepy so I guess I'll stop for tonight. Good night, see you in my dreams as always.

Good morning, how are you feeling this morning? I am feeling good as ever, but don't think I will husk corn today. My wrist is just too sore yet to husk. I don't know why it has to stay so sore when I have so much husking to do yet. Johnny and I will probably husk some on Saturday if my wrist is okay by then.

My folks and I talked this morning about making a frolic next Tues and Wed, so we might be done husking by the time you get here next week.

I guess we can talk better then I can write. This will be the last letter you will get from me till we meet again next week, but

I am looking for a letter from you. Wishing you God's richest blessing until we meet again. Hope to be seeing you soon. Love, Luck, and Best Wishes, Bye-Bye.

From a true Loving Sweetheart,

Amos J. Miller

Susie wrote a letter to Amos on December 7th. Amos received this letter before Susie received his December 5th letter!

Dec. 7, 1957

Dearest Loved Sweetheart,

Greeting of my Best Love to you. Will tonight try to scribble a few lines for you. I was kind of disappointed today that I didn't get any letter, but I am looking forward to getting one Monday. I suppose yours didn't get through in two days again.

How does this find you in the line of health? Me, I am just so common. There is some cold around here, but I don't have much of one. Hope you are fine and dandy sweet as candy. Would be sorry to hear different. Well, I suppose you wonder why I am writing if I haven't had your letter yet, but you will find out in a few more words. Now I hope it won't make you sick, when you read these words. I am almost afraid to write it. Well, I guess I might just as well write it and get it over with. I have changed plans again as to coming up there. But it is for the better instead of worse. ha Might just as well have a little joke in with it. ha May not be quite as hard to take.

Well, anyway here goes. I have decided to leave Trenton Wednesday evening, Dec. 11th. That will be next Wednesday evening, so I want you to meet me in Hazleton Thursday evening Dec. the 12th at 4:00 PM. Will be there one day sooner. I said it was for the better didn't I? ha Anyway, I wouldn't have had to write the way I did, but bet I had you feeling I wasn't coming, gel?

But you know who wrote this and you can see how mean I feel since I am almost to see you again. Anyway if nothing happens between now and then.

Well, this is Saturday evening ten minutes to eight. I am ready to go to bed, but the others aren't. Thought I would start your letter tonight.

What will you be doing tomorrow? Guess I'll go to church at Chester Gingerich's. We can just walk and boy that's going to be nice for tomorrow evening. We can just walk home after the Singing too. Hope it won't rain or get too cold.

Say about next Sunday. I don't know what to say, but I didn't want to go to church next Sunday. I know it is your church but oh well, I guess we can talk about that when I am there. Talking goes better than writing.

Well, what have you been doing these days? I suppose picking corn. I picked 1 1/2 days. You wonder why I didn't pick more--Gel? Well, my arms didn't stand it. I picked corn all day Tuesday and my left arm still hurts a little, but not very much.

Well, Darling, guess I'll stop for tonight because I can't think of more to write so good night.

Sweet dreams. Oh, yes, the other night I dreamed that you and I were neva hoche*[witness couple]* in somebody's wedding. Don't know whose it was. Levi just now said it is snowing. Say, I thought of something else. I hope you will come in the top buggy to meet me at Hazleton. That way the people won't all know as soon as I am there.

This is now schund Sunday evening after the Singing. I came home about 10 minutes ago. I didn't have to walk after all. There were some of the kids kind enough to give us a lift home.

Boy, it is really cold tonight. It would have been pretty cold to walk home, but anyway we didn't have to walk. This morning when we got up there was a blanket of about two inches of snow on the ground. But most of it is melted by now.

I wonder if you are home from the Singing already? I don't suppose so though because it is only about 10 minutes until 11:00. I thought I would write tonight because I want to leave early in the morning to go do Ezra's washing. Boy, I have so much work to do I am afraid I'll hardly get everything done that I want to do, but maybe if I work fast enough I will.

I sure had to take a lot of teasing today. It seemed like everybody knew I am leaving for Iowa again. Boy, just think of it just four more days and we will see each other again if nothing happens which I hope doesn't. These last few days sure seem to go slow. I guess I am in too big a hurry. I wouldn't have to be so silly, but so I am and seems I can't help it. But anyway, Darling, I hope you will overlook that.

Well, I was in church today and such a small church. It wasn't so small for a long time already. Well, you won't be getting such a big letter from me this time because it seems I can't write so much if I haven't had your letter yet to answer your questions.

Oh yes, we had some company tonight. Who do you think it was? Well I'll tell you , it was Ezras. They were here for supper. I suppose you will think such writing when you read this letter, gel?

It is now 11:00 and I am still not finished with this letter. You aren't home from the Singing yet I bet. Should be in bed already. Have to start catching up with my sleep, but I have only two nights, but I don't care. The sooner I see you again the happier I will be. Don't you think so?

Now don't forget to come to Hazleton Thursday 4:00 PM. Oh I know you won't forget because if you did I would know that you didn't love me very much. Don't you think so?

But anyway my news is all so I guess I'll stop for tonight. May know enough in the morning to fill this sheet. Good night Sweet Dreams. I'll be seeing you in my dreams again tonight.

Good morning, how are you this morning? I am just as usual.

Boooo, it is really cold this morning. Well, I don't know just how cold it is, but it seems cold. I am in a hurry and I don't have much time, so I will close. wishing you God's Richest Blessings. God be with you until we meet again.

With Luck, Love, and Best Wishes,

From a True Loving Sweetheart, Susie Ann Miller

✧ ✧ ✧

After receiving a letter like this who wouldn't be on cloud nine—or ten? It was another reminder how Susie's thoughts and my thoughts were so often the same.

She wrote to use the top buggy to meet her, and she didn't have my letter yet. I had written that I would use the top buggy so people couldn't see who it was.

It was a blessing to love someone who thought and loved the same way you did. This will be the last chapter of our courtship with letters. From here on it will be by memory that the Lord will provide. May God's blessing continue in the future chapters.

Chapter 23

# Susie Comes to Iowa

The big day finally dawned for Susie to arrive in Iowa. The snowflakes that drifted down on Amos that morning had brought with it some memories of Susie and her purest love! Yes, what a perfect day to meet her with this pure white snow falling ever so lightly. Amos's heart was filled with joy as he helped with chores that morning.

The corn had been husked with help from neighbors and friends the last two days. Amos wanted this day to go so fast, but he knew he needed to be patient once more.

"Amos, you're not eating much this morning," his mother said at the breakfast table.

Amos had been so deep in thought, he hadn't noticed his mother was talking directly to him. He sat in a daze—picking at his food.

John and Susan looked at each other and grinned. How well they remembered their days of courtship.

"Amos?" she tried again.

"What Mom?" Amos answered, coming back to reality.

Smiling she answered, "I said you're not eating very much this morning."

"I'm not?" Amos asked. He hadn't noticed.

John and Susan grinned at Amos, and he blushed a little. He knew what was on their minds.

At three that afternoon, Amos hitched up the horse and started out for Hazleton. He knew he would get there a little early, but he wanted to wait for her.

As the bus came into view, Amos's heart was beating fast. Finally—finally—finally was all he could think.

When Susie stepped down from the bus, Amos was right there. They hugged each other and their love was indescribable. What an exciting moment! Amos carried her suitcase to the buggy, then asked, "Would you like to go get a cup of coffee and something to eat before we head home?"

"Would anyone see us, do you think?" Susie asked.

"I doubt that anyone would be there," Amos assured Susie. So it was decided they would get that cup of coffee. When they got in the restaurant, they saw an Amish man sitting there, but Amos said it wasn't anyone he knew.

They stayed for nearly an hour and then headed on home. Susie was a little nervous about facing Amos's parents. Would they accept her as their future daughter-in-law?

"Have your mom and dad accepted that we're getting married?" she asked Amos.

"Honey, they don't talk about it to me, but I think they will, once we're together more," Amos answered.

Arriving home, Amos helped Susie down from the buggy. Then he said, "You just go on in, and I'll bring your suitcase after I put the horse in the barn." Susie would have preferred to wait on Amos, but didn't want to speak against him, so she said, "Okay, but hurry." Then she smiled.

"Don't you worry—I will!"

When Susie came up the walk to the door, Susan was at the door to greet her. She held the door open and said, "Just come right on in." They shook hands and found conversation to come easily. And that was the way Amos found them when he came in, both seemed to be enjoying themselves. Relief showed in Amos.

Amos helped finish up chores while Susie helped Susan finish up the supper.

"Now here seems to be a nice girl," thought Susan as they worked alongside each other. She was glad for her son's choice.

After supper, Susan said to Susie, "Now don't worry about the dishes, Johnny and Joni can wash them."

The boys both looked up and gasped. "What?" they both said as they looked at each other. They both were thinking, "We've finally got a girl around to do dishes, and then mom excuses her!" They weren't too happy about it.

Amos and Susie shelled popcorn for a while after supper. Susan had wanted it shelled before they moved to Missouri, so they needed to get at it. After a while, they went upstairs to catch up on some hugging and personal talk.

It didn't seem long until Amos's mother called, "Amos, we're ready for prayer." So they went on down and joined the family in the evening prayer. They went back upstairs to the room that Susie would sleep in. It was quite late when Amos's mother hollered upstairs, "Amos, I think it's time to get to bed."

"Oops," looking at the clock, they couldn't believe the time—1:00 a.m.! How time flies when you're having fun!

The next morning, it was easy getting up, knowing Susie was there. Amos worked outside that day while Susie helped his mother in the house. Amos made several trips to the house that morning on break. It was decided Susie would spend a few days at the Miller's, then help at Emanuel's the next week.

Amos and Susie skipped church on Sunday. Sunday evening, they spent with Emanuels and then went to the Singing. Amos took Susie back to Emanuel's. It was hard to leave her and go on home. It was decided he would come back to Emanuel's on Thursday evening.

Christmas was only a week away. They were both looking forward to their first Christmas together. Amos couldn't wait to see Susie's response to her gift.

Money wasn't easily earned, just working on the farm. Amos had asked his dad for money to buy his gal a gift and his response was, "Amos, I'll give you one cent for every bushel of corn you pick."

Amos didn't think that would amount to very much—but, oh well, that was better than nothing. After a lot of hard work picking each ear of corn by hand, Amos had picked 1800 bushels when they were done. That was $18. Wow! Amos was tickled pink. He spent $12 on a set of dinner dishes, white with gold trim. That left Amos with $6.

Susie was very happy with her gift.

Now it was Amos's turn to open his gift. He was surprised to open a new pair of leather gloves. Susie said, "I thought you could use them when driving in the open buggy. I know it gets pretty cold in zero weather."

Christmas was past before they knew it, and only a few days left before the sale. Amos helped his dad while Susie helped

Amos's mother bake pies, rolls, and bread to sell. The day of the sale, they made hot chocolate, coffee, and sloppy-joes. Susie helped sell the food and drinks on sale day.

They planned to load truck on January 23rd, so there was a lot of packing to do.

Susie left a few days after the sale. The excitement of moving helped Amos to pass the time. Knowing it wouldn't be long now until they would live in the same community and see more of each other also helped.

A few weeks later, John received a birthday card from Susie. The card meant a lot to John. He was thankful for his son's choice in seeking a partner.

Susie had written on the card:

Es ist besser for unrecht leiden,<br>
Den mit recht streiten.

*[It is better to bear with the unrighteous,*<br>
*And to stride with the righteous.]*

Chapter 24

# The Move to Missouri

Everyone got up early the day of moving. Neighbors had come by to help load. Amos was so excited about leaving. They left at 7:30 that evening with Emanuel and Amos riding with the semi. It was quite an experience to ride so high in the tractor and to be on the road with such a big rig. They drove to Ottumwa, Iowa, then stopped at a truck stop for a bite to eat, and headed out again. They arrived in Jamesport the next morning around eight. People had been waiting there to help unload the semi—including Susie. It only took a few hours to unload. Beds were set up and the women put the sheets and blankets on. Dressers were carried in and boxes unpacked to fill the drawers. Amos always figured if they're moving further south the weather should be warmer. It ended up being 21 degrees colder than Iowa! Amos had a warm feeling just knowing he was close to Susie. This was a new beginning for him.

Sunday after church, Amos had gone to Susie's place and spent the evening there. The evening came to a close too soon for Amos, but he knew he couldn't stay late for there were busy days ahead.

They didn't have a barn, so Amos spent time in the woods cutting pole trees to build a barn. The rickety old barn that had been there had fallen to pieces. They tore the metal off and used it on the new pole barn. While Amos worked on the poles, John worked on building a harness shop basement, building it into a hill. So the weeks following kept everyone busy.

Spring had finally arrived. They managed to get a few crops in, between their building.

Andy had been living in Ohio at the time of this move. He wrote a letter home saying he was going to Iowa to visit Emanuels, and would go on down to Missouri and stay home for a while.

Andy had come in time to help finish the buildings. During this time, an English neighbor came by and asked John if Amos could help him on the farm. He had 1000 acres of river bottomland. He offered to drive Amos back and forth every day and would pay him $25 a week. John gave his okay for Amos to go. The harness shop had been completed, but business hadn't picked up yet. They could use the money.

Not long after that, Andy worked out at Rayburn Tollen's. That left Johnny and Joni to help at home. The boys were still attending school so that left only evenings and Saturdays to help.

Sometimes Amos worked until two o'clock in the morning, plowing. And there wasn't any extra pay for the long hours. He was glad when the weekends came so he could rest up.

Amos and Susie had a lot of planning to do for their fall wedding. A few days later he received a letter from Susie.

Feb. 10,1958
Monday Morn. Blue Monday ha

Hi there Sweetheart,

Suppose you wonder why you get a letter from me today. Ike and two Bowling Green boys stopped here awhile ago and said there is a taffy pulling at Chester Gingerich's Tuesday evening. I didn't know if they would let you know or not so thought I would scribble a few lines for you being you weren't in a taffy pulling yet here.

They usually take something along. It doesn't make any difference which - - either a pint cream, a pint sugar, or a pint white Karo syrup. Now don't bring all three, just one, whichever suits you best.

Honey, you can then stop here and get me. Suppose Sadie will also go with us. Levi will probably just walk up. They usually try to be there by 8:00 PM. I just figured if you stop and take me along I can then take your things in with me. When we had a taffy pull in November, the boys went after their girls to bring them here, and they also took them home. But we could wait until some of the others leave and see if they do it that way, then we can too. But I know they will because they usually do.

Your Sweetheart,
Susie Ann Miller

After getting the letter about the taffy pulling, Amos was so excited. Amos enjoyed that evening. Everyone took some taffy home with them. Best of all, he got to see Susie again!

**Farm in Jamesport, MO**

Chapter 25

# The Summer of 1958

It was another nice spring day with the fieldwork coming along well. Amos was working for Junior Dixon, a neighbor. The spring rains had held them back for a while. During that time Amos had helped work on the equipment—packing wheel bearings, changing oil in the tractors and combine. They also cut down trees in the pasture and cleared land for more pasture.

By April they started the planting of beans and corn, so that meant extra hours of labor. The beef cattle had begun calving, and Junior bought some sows. By late May, Junior decided they should milk cows. He asked Amos one day, "Say Amos, how would you like to go to the Cameron sale and help pick out some dairy cows?"

"Oh, sure," came Amos's answer.

He then put Amos in charge of milking. One day soon after the cows were purchased, Amos decided to have a talk with Junior about his marriage.

"Er, m-m-em . . . " Amos cleared his throat. "Junior, I guess I'm planning on getting married this fall."

"What?" came the astonished farmer's voice. "Don't tell me."

"Just thought I'd let you know beforehand," said Amos.

"Are you still planning on working for me though?"

"I guess that depends on the pay," answered Amos. "Could I expect a raise?"

After some thought Junior said, "Amos, I wish I could, but right now I can't. I have a house you could live in, plus I could give you a half a gallon of milk a day plus two dozen eggs a week. Also I could give you half a hog a year for meat."

This didn't sound too bad to Amos. "I'll need to talk it over with my girlfriend first, then I'll let you know."

Amos and Susie talked it over that weekend and decided to take up the offer.

They went to take a look at the house. No one had lived there for three years so it was going to need some cleaning. A railroad ran close by. The track was on high ground, as high up as the house roof. "I think Mom and Sadie would help me clean it up," said Susie.

Amos needed to be baptized before he got married. So that spring he and Andy along with Ike Gingerich started taking instructions for baptism. They always went with the ministers in a private room, usually an upstairs room, for counseling. Two articles were read each time. Eighteen articles meant they needed to go for instructions nine times.

The ministers would admonish these young people in their beliefs, quoting Scriptures as to why they held on to their beliefs as they did. The other two boys had a time following the instructions. They both had shorter hair cuts than was allowed and clothes that weren't allowed.

When it came close to baptizing, the ministers counseled about waiting to baptize until two weeks later. By now Amos and Susie were getting nervous about this as this could interrupt their plans for marriage . . . Would they have to wait until a later date?

The next Sunday, Andy and Ike never showed up. They had decided to quit the instructions. Maybe it wasn't time for them to join yet. It was hard on Amos to see the other two boys drop out, but he also knew they needed to be at peace to go on. He prayed for the boys as he continued to go for instruction. Amos was baptized.

Amos received a letter from Susie.

Tuesday morning

Dear Sweetheart,

Greetings of purest love to you. I suppose you wonder why I am writing you a letter this morning. Well, I'll tell you. Sadie, Levi, and I just talked about Thursday. We hoped it would suit you and Andy to be at Kimberley's corner by 8:30 Thursday morning. We also want to be there by that time. Then I'll go with you because you will probably want to let your horses rest a little before we go on. It will probably be about 9:30 till we get to Ezra's then.

We want to leave Ezra's at 10:00, won't have too much time there. I want to send this letter with Levi to town so hope you will get it today yet. Don't forget your wieners and buns for Thursday evening.

Excuse me for scribbling what I have scribbled, but you had better just come on in here to our place so that we can put your wieners and buns in our refrigerator until evening. So be sure to drive in. We will wait here at home until you come. See you Thursday.

From your Loving Sweetheart,
Susie Ann Miller

✧ ✧ ✧

Their way of communication was strictly by mail. There were no phones to pick up, dial a number, and say, "Hello" and give your reason for calling.

The wiener roast was to be on "Old Christmas" which was the traditional Amish Christmas Day. The young folks had gathered at the park that day for the wiener roast.

✧ ✧ ✧

August was here now with the baptism in the past, and the wedding in the near future.

One morning, Amos decided to write Susie a letter.

Aug. 20, 1958

Good morning,

How are you feeling this morning? For me, I am pretty good, but can't see very good this morning. A bunch of bumble bees came after me yesterday and one stung me on my eyelid.

Well, you probably wonder why I am writing this morning or scribbling. Well, here it goes. I found out last night that it isn't this Saturday that we have to go to Tobe's it's next Sat. in a week. So thought I'd let you know to see if you still want to go to church next Sunday at Joe Bontrager's or not. If you do let me know, it makes me no difference. Maybe I should go and watch so I know how to act Sunday in a week. But, I don't have to go if you don't want to. If you want to go and Levi and Sadie don't go, let me know your answer in your letter.

If you want to go I will be over early Sunday morning to pick you up. Mother asked me if we had planned on going together, then I told her we hadn't yet. But I'd like to if it's okay with you. I have some things I'd like to tell you.

I wish I'd know how you feel about this, as far as going together to go to the other church district. Talking would always go better, but I was afraid your folks wouldn't like it if I came over one night during the week. So be sure to write me a letter so I know what you want to do Sunday.

I should be going to work as we got 300 bales of hay to unload this morning. So must hurry and get to work. Hope to be seeing you Sunday morning. So long.

From Your True Loving Sweetheart
Amos Miller

Following is Susie's response to Amos's letter of August 20, 1958.

Aug. 20, 1958

Hi there,

Got your letter today so guess I'll answer it tonight because I won't have time in the morning. Hope you can see better by the time you get my letter or you may not be able to read it. Next time you better leave the bumble bees alone. ha Am sorry though that it happened because I know how it feels.

I just wish you would have come up one evening but guess this will do. Boy these flies -- they are buzzing around here like 60.

About going to church Sunday. I guess I'll go anyway being church is at Joe Bontrager's. Sure would like to go with you to church but it is no use to think anything like that because my folks won't let us go together. Of course either Sadie or Levi will go or Mother and Father. So I'll have a way to go . But still hope to see you in church too.

Guess we will just have to leave right after the Singing so we will have plenty of time to talk. You can tell me then what you all have to tell me. I am really anxious to know! I can hardly wait till Sunday evening comes now.

Boy, I sure hope Tobe will have ordnung gma and gros gma right away. Guess if that Sunday would be gros gma we could still be published then. Guess what I want to do tonight yet? Well, I want to finish copying my recipes. Mother and Sadie went to Jamesport so I am here by myself. Oh yes, I can tell you something, but you daren't tell anybody. Guess Sadie is leaving next week for Clark, Missouri. She wants to work over there until our wedding. Lydia Mae will go with her. Guess Lydia Mae will be back before Sunday. They want to leave next Tuesday morning. Well my sheet is full so guess I'll have to stop for des mol. Have lots to tell you Sunday evening when we can be alone.

From Your True Loving Sweetheart,
Susie Ann Miller

Amos was glad to receive Susie's letter but wasn't glad to hear that he couldn't pick her up to go to Church with him, but he didn't want to go against her folks' wishes. He loved Susie too much and didn't want her folks to get upset with him before they got married.

They both wanted to be in the other church district that Sunday as their friend Eli Detwelier and his gal were supposed to get published to be married that day. That's what Amos was saying in his letter, "Maybe I should go and watch . . ." He wanted to know how to act when they were published in two weeks. They did have ordnung gma *[church council meeting]* before they were published to be married. It was only a few weeks after that when they had gros gma *[communion church]*. So their wedding plans were working out as they had hoped.

About a week before they were published to be married, Susie came down to Amos's folks. Helen Dixon was taking them to Chillicothe to get their blood tests and to apply for their marriage license. Helen was the wife of Junior Dixon, the English man Amos worked for.

When they got to the corner, Amos saw Eli Borkholder coming down the hill with the wagon. Amos told Susie to lie down in the back seat so Eli couldn't see that she was with him.

Eli might tell somebody else. After they turned the corner and were aways down the road, Susie sat back up again. The problem was, Eli got to the corner too soon and saw Susie sit back up. They didn't know at the time whether Eli had seen Susie or not, but found out soon enough.

The following Sunday was when they were published to be married. When Eli got to Church that Sunday morning, he asked Amos who his passenger was in the backseat–the one who sat up. Of course, Amos didn't have to tell him—Eli had a good idea! Eli asked, "Amos, is there going to be a wedding published today?" Amos told Eli he could think whatever he wanted to. Well, Eli just couldn't keep his big mouth shut, he had to tell the other boys that he's sure Amos and Susie will be published to be married today.

So naturally after the announcement of their wedding, when Amos went out to hitch up his horse, he found out quick enough what the boys had in mind. They had knotted up the neck rope on his horse to delay Amos and Susie from leaving before Church let out—so they could come out and tease them. Well, Amos fixed them! Instead of spending a lot of time getting the knots open, he just got his bridle and unsnapped the neck rope from the horse—and left the knotted-up neck rope there till later on.

Needless to say Amos was pretty upset with Eli for saying something about it to the young boys. To think Eli was a preacher! This was very improper because preachers are supposed to keep a secret and be trusted. It took Amos quite awhile to get over Eli's behavior. He lost any trust that he had for him. Amos did talk to Eli and let him know he didn't think it very nice of him, revealing this kind of information.

The last letter Susie wrote to Amos before they were married . . .

Sept. 17, 1958

Dearest Sweetheart,

Greetings of Love. How are you this morning? I am just as usual except a little cold. It sure seems good to see the sun again this morning. I hope it warms up and dries up today again. Boy, we really have the mud again this week. If the sun shines all day like it looks that it may, it will be pretty well dried up by tonight.

What are you doing this week? Me, well I washed yesterday and got my comforter ready to put in frame. So I want to finish that this week, and I also want to finish my bed today. I have to give it a coat of varnish yet, then it is ready.

I suppose you wonder why you are getting this letter, gel? Well, I'll tell you. I would like for you to bring that bushel of apples up one evening. Your mother said they have a bushel we can have if we want them. I told her we would take them, but they should be sorted because those that we have here are starting to rot. So I just thought I would tell you to bring them up. So I am hoping to see you either Thursday or Friday evening. Well Levi is ready, so must hike as I want to send this with him to the mailbox. I will be looking for you.

From your true Loving Sweetheart,
Susie Ann Miller

After receiving a letter like this, Amos didn't need the second invitation to take those apples up. This just gave them another chance to be together during the week. Even with the wedding being only about three weeks away, it was getting harder to be apart for a whole week. So in the weeks ahead, he usually found some reason to go up and see Susie during the week.

Susie, her mother, and Sadie went down to the house they were going to move into and cleaned it up and also did some painting. So naturally, Amos had to stop in there on his way home from work to check them out to see if they needed anything. These times together gave Susie and Amos a chance to discuss more wedding plans.

In the next few weeks, they had to make more plans as to who was going to be their neva hoche *[witness as best man and bridesmaid]*. They also had to choose who they were going to have for table waiters. Some of Susie's cousins from Wisconsin and also some of Amos's cousins from Indiana would have different parts in their wedding.

The plans were coming along fine until they told Susie's folks they were inviting some aunts, sisters, and brothers who weren't Amish. Their response was really a disappointment to Susie and to Amos. Susie and Amos talked it over and decided if they can't invite those who aren't Amish, they would tell her folks to forget about their wedding plans. If they can't invite them, they will just go to the Justice of the Peace and get married—they won't need to have the wedding at their house.

This changed Susie's folks' minds as they wanted them to have a wedding instead of just getting married at the Justice of the Peace. So Susie's parents agreed they could invite those who weren't Amish to their wedding.

Now Amos and Susie thought things were going to work out the way they had planned. There were still a lot of things to do before the wedding.

Then three days before the wedding, they got word from Indiana that Amos's uncle Emanuel passed away suddenly with a heart attack. Two days before the wedding, Amos's dad and two of his brothers went to Indiana for the funeral. They came back the night before the wedding.

This was quite a challenging time for Susie and Amos to go through. They had to find someone else for table waiter because one of Uncle Emanuel's boys was to be one of their table waiters. Amos's cousin Emanuel couldn't be at their wedding because of his dad's passing away so suddenly.

Amos and Susie had to spend a couple of evenings going to different places to find another person to be table waiter. Susie and Amos had their first disagreement on one of those evenings. Amos wanted to ask a different guy than Susie did. Guess they were both quite tense—sudden changes to make three days before their wedding! Who wouldn't be tense?

Amos and Susie ended up telling each other that it didn't make any difference who they got for the replacement. The important thing was that they loved each other and wanted to spend their lives together. They compromised so they could continue their wedding as planned.

Now they thought they had everything planned and another thing came up. Amos's twin brother, Andy, wanted to have Susie's sister, Sadie, as his partner—and they had different plans. They had planned for Susie's cousin from Wisconsin to be Andy's partner.

Andy said he wouldn't be Amos's best man unless he could have Sadie as his partner. Andy and Sadie had been dating a few times, and they had a crush on each other. After some talking with Andy, he finally agreed to having Susie's cousin as his partner, but he wasn't going to have a date with her! Amos and Susie said this was okay with them.

As it turned out guess "she wasn't too bad" as Andy ended up having a date with her! Amos and Susie were relieved when Andy said he enjoyed himself. It was just that he had never met her cousin before the wedding.

So now their plans were finally finalized—just the night before their wedding. You can imagine how much sleep they got that night! But they had the next morning to look forward to—the first day of their future together.

Chapter 26

# Wedding — Our First Child

On the morning of October 23, 1958, there was a nice sunrise. It looked like they were going to have a nice wedding day. Amos and Susie were a little nervous, but they loved each other very much. Now all they had to do was to think of the future they would have together—that would calm their nerves and put joy in their hearts.

Amos and some of the rest of the wedding party had stayed at Susie's house the night before the wedding. The time finally came for them and their witnesses to go to the wedding church. They had escorts to take each of the couples down to the church. Susie's brother, Junior, was escort driver for the couple.

Amos and Susie were finally seated on the front row next to the preacher's bench and waiting for 9:00 a.m. when the services were to start. Finally, the singing began, and the preachers went to the upper room.

Then it was time for Susie and Amos to get up to go to the upper room where the preachers were. With his legs shaking, with Susie at his side, Amos made it to the upper room.

There the preachers counseled them, telling them what they should do and not do as they began their future together. They also advised them how they should spend their first night together as husband and wife. They would be blessed by following the rules of the Bible and also their beliefs as they were informed to live by. After being in the upper room for half an hour, Amos and Susie were dismissed to go back down again. The preachers came down about ten minutes later.

Then the wedding sermon began which lasted about two and a half hours. Amos knew that Amish preachers always tried to marry a couple at 12:00 noon. He wasn't sure why—was this a tradition or were there biblical reasons?

The time finally came when the preacher asked Amos and Susie if they still felt like they expressed themselves in the upper room, if so, they should come forward at this time. As they stood up to go forward, their witness couples–the best man and his partner, the bridesmaid and her partner—stood up with them and remained standing until the ceremony was over. Then Amos and Susie and their witness couples all sat down at the same time

When the ceremony was over, the preacher would ask for zeigness [if everyone was in agreement]. After that as the church started singing, Amos and Susie with their wedding party left to go to Susie's folks for the wedding dinner. When all those attending the wedding had arrived, they would sit down to eat.

They did not have enough tables for all to be seated as Susie's folk's house was kind of small, so some had to wait to eat until the second time around. By this time it was about two-thirty, and the old folks started singing for the wedding party. They sang about a half hour.

Amos and Susie finally had free time to leave the table till the evening meal for the young folks. They visited with their guests and also received their wedding gifts. By the time Susie and Amos went upstairs to their room, they had only a few hours to relax before the evening meal with the young folks.

After supper, the young folks sang for a little over an hour. Then after picking on the newly married couple, the usual teasing, they started to leave to go home.

Finally about 11:00 p.m., Amos and Susie got to go to bed. They were both quite tired out after their big day! The bad part was they didn't have a room all to themselves as their brother-in-law and his wife also slept in the same room. So this was quite a way to spend their wedding night with someone else in the same room. What a honeymoon!

The next morning after breakfast, it was time to start washing all the wedding dishes. Amos and Susie, their witness couples, and whoever else was around all helped to clean up. By mid-afternoon they had things cleaned up and a wagon loaded with their things to move to their own house. It was late evening by the time Amos and Susie had most things unpacked and a bed set up so they could spend the night in their new home.

On Saturday morning, Amos hired a guy with a truck to go to an estate auction. They needed a dinette table and chairs. Also their own bed as they had just borrowed a bed from Susie's folks. Amos also bought a red chest at the sale (which he still has). They used it to pack dishes in when they moved.

Then they stopped to get groceries on the way home. It seemed like there was a lot to buy for the first time. After they unloaded everything, Amos paid the driver $6. They had $2.85 left to their name. It would be three weeks before Amos got paid as he had drawn two weeks pay in advance to help pay for the wedding expenses. So this was the start for their future together.

The reason he had to draw two weeks pay in advance was because he got married before he was twenty and his folks were getting all the money he made.

After they were married he was to pay his folks $50 each month until he paid them $500. This is the amount they figured he would have brought home for them if he would have waited until he was 20 years old to get married.

Amos was making $25 a week working on the farm, this left them with $50 per month for themselves after he paid his folks $50. Now Amos loved his parents very much, but he sure didn't think this was fair as he had worked out for his parents since he was thirteen years old and gave them all the money he earned. Guess he always had too big a heart to keep some of the money for himself as some of his brothers did. He figured all those years should count for something and that he shouldn't have to keep giving them money after he was married.

They kept giving them $50 per month until they found out that Susie was pregnant. Susie said that they should go up some evening and talk to his folks about that $50 a month. Susie said they needed some money to buy material to make dresses for their new baby. Susie said she wasn't going to have a baby and no clothes to put on her! He agreed with Susie and so they went up to his folks one night and let them know how they felt. He told his folks with a family coming on they had their own life to lead and needed their money they earned to meet their expenses. So finally his folks said it was okay if they didn't pay them fifty dollars a month but that the balance of the $500 would be deducted from their inheritance when that time came. He told them he didn't care if that is the way they want to do it. He asked them how they figured they would make it in the future if they didn't have more than $50 income each month.

Amos also informed them that after all these years he would think they could make it on their own without his $50 per month. He reminded them that the last six years he gave all his money home to them and didn't complain, by doing this he sure didn't expect them to ask for $500 until he was twenty years old. He didn't think his folks were too happy with them that night, but Susie and Amos felt better after having expressed their feelings. His parents did congratulate them on their new family coming on, and they left on good terms.

Susie was so happy when she found out she was pregnant. She wanted children so much. For a while she thought she wouldn't be able to get pregnant, and she was on the unhappy side. Susie's dream finally came true in what she wanted out of life. She wanted to be married and raise a family.

It wasn't hard to know what to make for the baby because all babies, boys and girls, wore dresses until they were a year old. It was easier to change their diapers that way. You can see why Amos fell in love with Susie because of the loving person she was.

As time went on, Susie got more excited about this firstborn baby they looked forward to have and hold, love and cherish. He would come home from work and Susie would show him a new dress she made for the baby. Then she knitted booties, then a blanket. Susie was so happy that she was always all smiles and eyes aglow when Amos came home. Then before long, he would come home and she would say how she felt the baby move and kick that day.

I guess all new parents look forward to having their firstborn. Susie was one of a kind with a love for Amos and her baby and children to come that is indescribable how she would just overflow with love and happiness.

Spring was here and the field work had started. Amos spent long hours plowing on the thousand acres of river bottomland that they farmed. Some nights Amos would plow till two in the morning. Susie wasn't too happy staying home by herself when he worked those long hours. Once the crops were in, they worked regular hours again. Of course farming hours are normally around fifty hours a week. Susie put out a garden, and they also got some baby chicks to raise as fryers. This gave Susie something to do besides housework.

Susie had the baby chicks in the yard below a big tree with netting in a big round circle to keep the chicks in—she would move them to different areas. One night when Amos came home Susie was in the yard by her baby chicks. She was all excited and also scared. She had heard the chicks making a noise and went out to see what was going on. To Susie's surprise, there was a big bull snake eating up her chicks. Susie grabbed a garden hoe and hit the snake to chase it away. As the snake went away, it crawled up the big tree into a large knothole which was about eight feet off the ground.

Susie told Amos what happened and asked him to get up in the tree and see if he could get the snake out and kill it before it ate more of her baby chicks. So he drove the tractor over next to the tree and stood on the rear tractor wheel so he could reach the hole where the snake had crawled in. There that snake was all coiled up in the hole, looking at him!

Amos didn't have any idea how large the snake was until he finally got it out of the hole after breaking the garden hoe handle! When he finally got the snake out and killed it, he laid it on the ground and stretched it out. He took his tape measure and measured the snake—it was nine and a half feet long. You could see four humps in the snake which were from the baby chicks it had swallowed.

This was the only time they had any snake come after their chicks. Susie kept a very close eye on her chicks after that. Once in a while, a cat would come around and try to get inside the netting to get the chicks. But Susie had a big stick which the cats didn't like very much and soon thereafter didn't bother them anymore. They had some very good fryer eating that summer.

Susie also was busy canning during the summer now. Susie would also go up to her mom's about once a week. Sometimes her mom and sister, Sadie, would come down and help Susie out with her canning. Being pregnant, Susie was limited to what she could do.

Sometimes in the mornings Susie would get a knock on the door and it would be a railroad bum wanting to know if she would make him some breakfast. Susie usually kept the screen door locked. Susie said she would make him breakfast. When she had it made she would come to the door and ask the bum to go over and sit on the big tree stump and she would set the food out on the porch and close the door then tell him he could come and get his breakfast.

Susie fed quite a few railroad bums while they were living there. One time one of them left $2 under the plate when he was done. Susie thought she made some big money and was excited to tell Amos when he came home. As fall came along, she had less bums to feed, guess it was too cold to ride the trains then.

The summer of 1959 was over already! Their first year together really went fast—the exciting thought of having a baby helped. It was around the first week in September, and Susie was getting closer to the time for the baby to be born. During this time Amos worked on the farms closer to home so he wouldn't be so far away when Susie needed him.

On the morning of September 15, Susie told Amos that today will probably be the day for their new arrival. Susie called the farm where Amos was working about eleven in the morning, and said she was having some sharp pains—that he should come home so they could go see Dr. Bailey at his clinic at Jamesport. Needless to say, it wouldn't take Amos long to get home as he was all excited—which is normal for a new expecting father.

Amos knew it was no use driving the tractor home, instead he asked Junior if he would take them up to the doctor. Junior said he didn't see any need for him to take off work. Amos could drive the truck just as good as he could. Amos was disappointed that Junior responded in this way. He knew that the Amish weren't supposed to drive trucks.

Amos didn't have much time or choice, so he took the truck home and took Susie up to the clinic. He did have a driver's license to drive but as far as the Amish were concerned, he was only to drive when they went from one river bottom field to another one. He didn't know what they would say if they saw him drive to town with Susie, but he had no time to wait. He wanted to get Susie there on time. Because of it being their first child, they didn't know how things would work out.

As it turned out they had plenty of time. Amos stayed with Susie the rest of the day and most of the night. Finally the doctor said that it would probably be tomorrow forenoon sometime as Susie's labor pains had subsided. So Amos went home and came back early the next morning. Susie was feeling fine the next morning, but hadn't had very many labor pains. So around nine that morning, the doctor gave her something to induce her labor pains.

Amos was with Susie all the time and around 11:00 a.m. on September 16, 1959, their firstborn arrived, a beautiful baby girl. They named her Sarah Ann because Susie's mother was Sarah and Susie's middle name was Ann. You talk about an experience of seeing your first child being born and being a new father and Susie, a new mother. They were very happy. They were very thankful for a healthy baby. Around 4 p.m., the doctor said Susie could go home. So proud papa took his beautiful wife and baby girl home.

Susie's sister, Sadie, helped Susie out a few days till Susie could take care of herself and little Sarah Ann. Susie's mother and Amos's mother were also down the next morning to help out and see their new granddaughter. Susie's mother was very happy they named their girl after her.

In the weeks ahead Susie was very happy to take care of her little daughter. Susie would always tell Amos how Sarah was that day, how much she slept, how content a baby she was. Sometimes Susie said that Sarah slept so much today that she hardly had any time holding her. Of course proud Papa would also have his turn holding his little daughter when he came home from the day's work. About the first three weeks they had a lot of company that came to see them and their little Sarah Ann. Susie and Amos were both pretty proud parents to show off their beautiful little Sarah. The days ahead were very enjoyable for them. Although their days ahead were enjoyable, they received some sad news from Iowa. The news was that Freddie Stutzman got killed in a car accident on Nov 13, 1959.

Amos told Susie that he wants to go to the funeral as Freddie and Eddie Stutzman were twins, and they also were their good friends as they had run around together. The Stutzman twins were only three months older than the Miller twins, Amos and Andy.

Freddie had a girlfriend, and they were planning to get married. This was quite shocking news to everybody.

Amos and Susie's little daughter Sarah was only eight weeks old at the time. They stopped over at Kalona, Iowa at Susie's sister Mattie's place overnight. The next morning they went on up to the funeral at Oelwein, Iowa.

Chapter 27

# First Farm — Our Second Child

Things were going well for Amos and Susie—a very exciting time. It seemed to them that their little Sarah Ann was growing so fast. During this time, they were also expecting their second child.

Farming wasn't going as good as it had been. As far as having days that Amos could take off, Junior wasn't as cooperative as he was when Amos first started to work for him. Susie and Amos discussed it at some length and decided to see what else would be available for them.

Then they found out about the Kimberley farm. The farmer also owned the newspaper print shop in Jamesport. He was trying to take care of the farm, but wasn't doing a very good job.

Amos found out the owner was looking for someone to take care of the Kimberley farm on shares. Amos and Susie looked into what he had to offer. The owner had a few cows he was milking. They were to get half of the milk income and also half of the crops and calves for taking care of the farm. They thought it sounded pretty good, and it would also give them an opportunity to start up their own farming.

Well, one thing Amos and Susie didn't know was how rundown the farm really was. The cattle would get out on a daily basis as the fence on the farm was really bad. Amos was fixing fence on a daily basis for a long time! The milk check wasn't very much as the cows were about all dried up. Their half was around $30 every two weeks.

Amos and Susie decided they had to do something else to go along with the farming till things got to going better. Amos found out there was an old house he could tear down and have all the lumber. So he spent around a month tearing down the house and bringing the lumber home. Amos then built a double farrowing hog house large enough for six sows.

Amos had gone to the bank before he did this, and the bank agreed to loan him money to buy some sows. The farm owner gave him permission to use a small field for his hogs. Amos started to raise weaning pigs. This was all for themselves—Mr. Kimberley didn't get anything out of this operation. The first gilts didn't do all that good, but the next round, the sows had an average of nine each.

During this time of fence fixing and building the hog house, Amos had his brother Johnny help him out. But it seemed like every time he needed help, his parents said they couldn't spare Johnny. So one time Amos told his mom, "I might as well be 1000 miles away, and I would get just as much help."

Soon after this time, Susie and Amos found out where there was a small farm for sale. They looked into buying it. They also talked to the bank to see if they could borrow the money to buy six good dairy cows. At this time, Simon Hochstetler was going to have a dairy sale and sell all his cows. He had a very good herd.

Susie and Amos did some serious figuring—they felt they could pay for the farm with the dairy cows and make a living off the weaning pigs. The bank said they would loan them the money, so they were quite excited about this.

Next they talked with both parents and told them about their plans. Well, guess this was the wrong thing to do! Both parents "popped their bubble" and said they couldn't make it—that they would be going too deep in debt. Needless to say, Susie and Amos went home very upset and not knowing what they should do. They were hoping their parents would encourage them and be happy for them.

After some time had passed, Amos and Susie discussed it just between themselves. They finally decided if their parents don't think they can make it, they will move to Indiana where Amos could work in a factory for an income.

When their parents found out they were planning to move to Indiana, it was their turn to be upset and to try to talk them out of it. But Amos and Susie had made up their minds—they were going to move no matter what the parents want to say about it.

Susie and Amos decided after the crops were in, they would have their sale so they could move by the end of October to Indiana. They started to make up a list for their sale. They had half of the crops and hay, and the calves. They also had their own sows and pigs plus their hog house, and the lumber that was left. They were surprised at how many things they had.

Amos had a frolic to clean up the rest of the lumber and also to finish off the hog house. The very same day, the veterinarian came out to test the cows.

Now this was a very busy day, but to top it off Susie had to go into labor pains. Both Mothers were there to be with her. They would call out and say, "Susie wants Amos in the house!" After about six times running back and forth, Amos had one of the other guys help the veterinarian with the cows.

Amos had already called the doctor when he put one of the other guys in charge of the cows. Amos had told the doctor he better come out as Susie's pains were very close together. When he got back in the house—he was only gone five minutes—Amos was told they had a new baby boy, their second child. Amos and Susie's son Jerry was born September 13, 1960.

The doctor didn't get there till half an hour after the baby was born. Amos told the doctor, "You didn't come when asked to come, so you didn't deliver our son, so I should have to only pay half price!" The doctor did agree with him and only charged Amos $50. Pretty reasonable, wouldn't you say?

Yes, this was quite a busy day for Amos. He was sure glad to retire for supper, and of course, cuddle his new son. Finally both mothers and all the help were gone home, and Amos and Susie were by themselves to enjoy their new son.

Everything was fine till around two in the morning, when their son started to cry. So Susie woke Amos up and said, "He probably is wet. Would you change his diaper?"

"Okay." Amos got up and started to change his son's diaper. Well, the baby wasn't just wet. He had his first bowel movement, black as could be. Amos got him cleaned up and had just put his new diaper down when here comes some more!

Susie thought it was funny, and she started laughing—just watching Amos trying to get his job done. Susie said, "It hurts to laugh, but I can't help it! It's quite a sight just to watch you." But at least the little fellow slept the rest of the night.

When morning came, Amos did his chores and cooked breakfast for his family. Then he worked on getting things ready for their sale which was coming up in about two weeks.

The sale was over, and things brought quite a bit of money. Amos and Susie were loading truck two days after the sale and getting ready to move to Indiana. They had a straight stock truck to move their things. Everything was put on the truck—household, the buggy and the horse—it was full!

Their son Jerry was six weeks old the day they left for Indiana. The whole family rode in the cab of the truck. There had been some sad good-byes from their parents, but they wished Amos and Susie the best.

On October 16, 1960, they arrived in Indiana—on the Harley Yoder farm east of the Mishler packing plant, southeast of Shipshewana. They would stay on Harley's farm for taking care of the chores and packing eggs.

Brother-in-law Harvey Miller lived a quarter mile down the road from them. The neighbors came and helped them unload the truck. Now they were getting settled in Indiana—no job yet, but debt free with about $500 left after the trucker was paid.

Amos and Susie were thankful they had a safe trip to Indiana. The future days would hold quite a few challenges for them.

Chapter 28

# Our Future in Indiana

Arriving in Indiana, Amos and Susie knew there would be some new adjustments. The children had done well while traveling. Sarah had a cold and was a little fussy. Jerry was well.

There was so much to do—they didn't know where to begin. Amos and Susie didn't unpack all their belongings, because they didn't plan to stay for long. They wanted to buy a place as soon as possible.

Harley Yoder came over the first morning and showed Amos around. Amos had some second thoughts after that. "Wow," he muttered to himself after Harley was gone. "That is a lot of chores." They had to gather eggs twice a day. Then wash up all the eggs in the evening, so they would be ready for the truck in the morning. Chores also included milking two cows and taking care of several horses.

Amos harnessed up Sylvia, their driving horse, to make a trip to town. Going back in the house, he needed to get Susie's shopping list. Susie stayed home because of Sarah's cold.

"Amos, don't you think we should write our folks to let them know we got here safe and sound?" Susie asked.

"Yes, that's probably a good idea," Amos answered.

So they both sat down and wrote letters to their parents. Amos took the letters to town and mailed them from there.

Sylvia was pretty stiff from the long trip to Indiana. By the time Amos got back from town, she had limbered up.

It was time to start chores. After supper, Amos and Susie helped each other clean the eggs.

"I'm going to need to look for a job soon, Susie," Amos said while filling the egg cartons. "Brother Harvey told me I might be able to get a job at Mishler's meat plant."

"Maybe you should go tomorrow and check it out," came Susie's reply.

The next morning Amos harnessed up the horse and went to seek a job. Mishler's offered him a job on the kill floor. Amos took the job and started the next day. With Amos working at his new job, Susie would gather the eggs.

What a new experience! Amos had to use a rifle to shoot large bulls in steel stanchions. About the time he was up on the platform aimed to shoot, the bulls would jump at him and scare him half to death. After the bulls were shot, Amos had three minutes to hang them by the hind legs and stick them. If he didn't get the legs up in time, the bulls would start kicking—and you'd better be out of the way! After a bull was hung, its front legs and head were removed. At first it took Amos 20 minutes to do this. After a while, he did it in 10 minutes.

The hogs were hung alive on the hoist, then stuck to bleed to death. From there, they went to the scalding tank, then rolled into a roller to remove the hair. On a good day, 7 beef and 15 to 20 hogs went through from 4:00 a.m. to 1:00 p.m. By then, you knew you had done a day's work

One night Amos confronted Susie, "You know Susie, my job is very dangerous. I don't feel comfortable working there. I think I'll look for some other work."

Amos soon found out about a job opening at Monteith in Shipshewana. He filled out an application. About a week later, he was hired to remove brake pads from brake shoes—which was a dirty job. But getting dirty didn't matter to Amos. Anything was better than shooting those bulls!

Monteith had offered him $2.75 an hour. That was an increase in pay, so Amos was happy about that.

Amos and Susie soon found out about a place near Goshen they could rent. They packed up and made another move. But finding a ride to Amos's work was complicated.

During a visit with his Uncle Andy, Amos was told about a job offer at Shasta Trailers. Uncle Andy was the assistant superintendent there. After inquiring about a job, Amos was hired a week later for $4.75 an hour. Things seemed to be getting better all the time.

Amos and Susie kept letters going to their parents, and they got letters in return. Their parents always mentioned how they missed the grandchildren, and hoped they would come visit sometime. Susie was expecting their third child now. How she wished she could talk to her mother. She was getting homesick by now. They were adjusting to all the new people at church.

Amos was experiencing new things at work and was concerned about raising his children right. He hadn't been taught to read the German Bible like Susie had. How was he going to teach his children to read the German Bible if he himself didn't know? Amos and Susie discussed and prayed about the situation. They talked to some other parents about their concern and found out they had the same concern for their children.

Amos and Susie would pray and wait for the answer.

## *Note to the Reader*

To find out how God intervened in the lives of Amos and Susie and what He had in store for them, read the next Amos & Andy book. Trying to live a lifestyle in keeping with the heritage in which they were brought up, the twins meet many trials and changes along the way.

Now at its beginning stage, the second Amos & Andy book will reveal 40 more years of the twins' life journey.

May the Lord bless you until then.

—Amos J. Miller
Goshen, Indiana